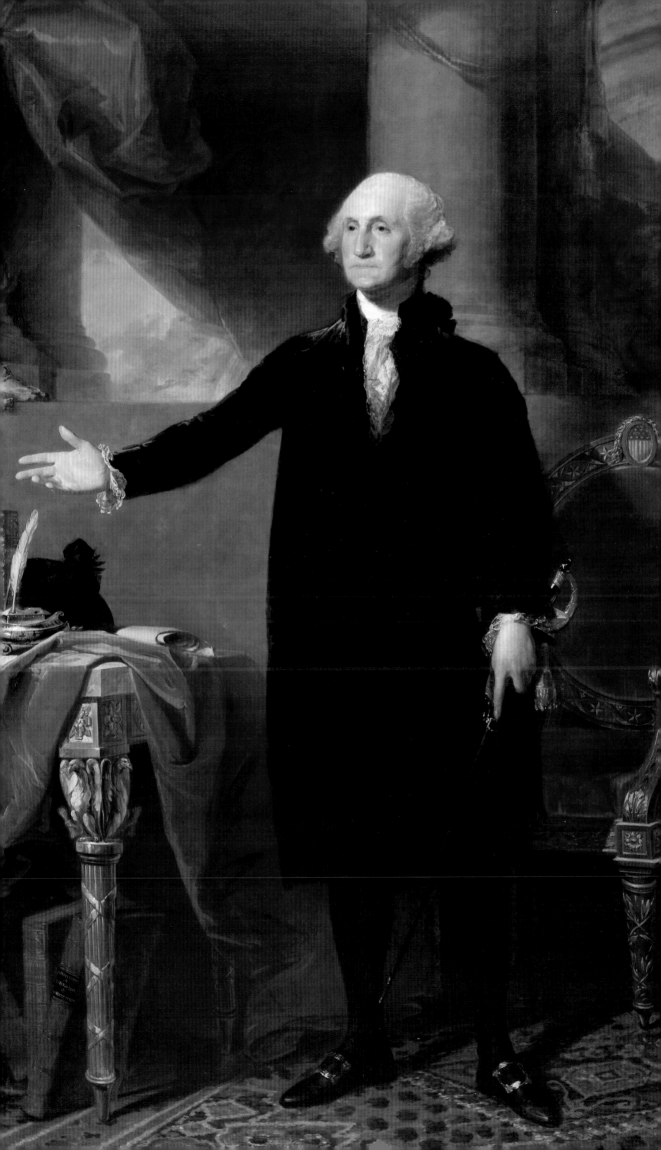

★ *George Washington: A National Treasure*

Foreword by Marc Pachter
With an introduction by Richard Brookhiser
And essays by Margaret C. S. Christman and Ellen G. Miles

National Portrait Gallery,
Smithsonian Institution
Washington, D.C.
In association with the
University of Washington Press
Seattle and London

This book and exhibition
have been made possible
through the generosity of the
Donald W. Reynolds Foundation.

Front and back covers
and half title page:
George Washington
(Lansdowne portrait)
by Gilbert Stuart.
Oil on canvas, 1796.
National Portrait Gallery,
Smithsonian Institution;
acquired as a gift to the nation
through the generosity of the
Donald W. Reynolds Foundation

Library of Congress Preassigned
Control Number: 2001098715

Edited by Dru Dowdy
Designed by Studio A,
Alexandria, Virginia
Printed by Schneidereith and Sons,
Baltimore, Maryland

Distributed by the
University of Washington Press
P.O. Box 50096
Seattle, WA 91845-5096
ISBN 0-295-98237-3 paper
ISBN 0-295-98236-5 cloth

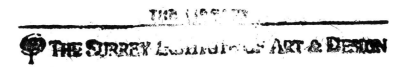

★ *Contents*

★ *Foreword*

I HAVE TO ADMIT THAT I ONCE TOOK THE GREAT LANSDOWNE portrait of George Washington for granted. When I arrived at the National Portrait Gallery in 1974 to take up my then-position as chief historian, the Gallery had already secured pride of place for the portrait, the first thing one saw after ascending the building's grand staircase to the second floor. It seemed right that Washington served as anchor of the nation's place for remembering the greatest Americans. As Gilbert Stuart portrayed him, his arm outstretched, a rainbow over his shoulder, our first President stood, the confident father of a confident nation.

The National Portrait Gallery had, in fact, "acquired" this founding icon of our nation only some six years before. I use quotation marks because it was only on long-term loan to the Gallery from the British aristocratic family that had owned it for more than three-quarters of a century. Why that was so, and why this greatest historical painting of America's origins had British owners since 1797, I leave to Margaret Christman's essay to reveal. But in any case, the painting had been in the United States since the opening of the National Portrait Gallery in 1968 and was likely, one thought, to remain in Washington, D.C., forever.

And then, in the fall of 2000, some three months after I had taken up the directorship of the National Portrait Gallery, the painting's presence could no longer be taken for granted. Lord Dalmeny, the young owner of the portrait, announced that he had decided to sell it, and soon. This was a surprise at a number of levels. The Smithsonian had attempted to purchase the portrait for years without success. Suddenly, we were in a race against time to buy it, for a price that, while appropriate given its unique value (indeed, far less than it might bring at auction), was a staggering $20 million. We were given about six months to find the money; then it would go to the highest bidder from wherever in the world.

It was time to take a closer look at this painting, to understand why its loss to the nation was literally unthinkable. The Lansdowne (named after the Englishman who received it as a gift in 1797) is not the greatest work of art ever produced by an American; it is not even the most accurate likeness of the President. Yet Gilbert Stuart had produced a George Washington for the ages, resolute in the face of the multiple crises of our nation's origins, grand in the tradition not of a king but of democracy's representative, civilian rather than military in his authority, and, above all, the embodiment of a nation both stable and free.

This is a painting that speaks to each American. It provides a way to think about a time when America's success was by no means certain, about a man whose traits of character became bound up with his nation's fate, about the expectation for our nation's highest office, the presidency, at the moment of its invention. There are so many ways to understand it. Ellen Miles tells us what we know about the time of its creation and the artist who produced it. Richard Brookhiser tells us

Third-grader John Collins sent a drawing for a proposed "Save George" website to the National Portrait Gallery during its campaign to raise money to purchase the Lansdowne painting.

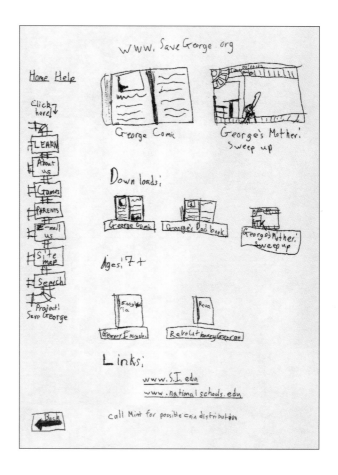

On March 14, 2001, the Washington Post *featured National Portrait Gallery Director Marc Pachter and the newly acquired Lansdowne portrait on its front page.*

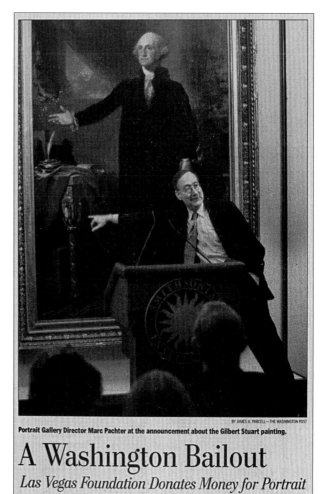

what one citizen of our own time has found in this remarkable painting to explain the nature of Washington and of the generation who forged with him our American identity. In it, each of us will find our own meaning.

This was a national treasure that had to be saved, but how? The sum was many times greater than the National Portrait Gallery's annual budget. When I took our problem to the country, in national and local newspapers and on television, the response was overwhelming. In one case, an entire school district–that of Pasadena, Texas–took up a collection; in another, a third-grader in upstate New York produced a design for a "Save George" website meant to appeal to children throughout the country. Had we the time, we might well have found the necessary money from twenty million Americans, each sending in one green "portrait of George Washington." But in the time we had, we needed a smaller number of Americans–one perhaps, or an organization–to save this painting for their countrymen and women. In one moving instance, a leader of the Vietnamese American community, in a gesture of gratitude to the nation, offered to raise the money. Clearly, this was more than just another valuable painting.

The day after my appearance on the *Today Show*, I heard from the Donald W. Reynolds Foundation of Nevada. Could I come to their offices in Las Vegas in a few days? Indeed I could, and on the morning of March 3, 2001, the foundation, in a remarkable act of patriotism and generosity, provided not only the necessary money to purchase the Lansdowne, but half again as much to provide for a national tour for the national treasure and a place to welcome it back to the National Portrait Gallery, where it would be available to future generations. It was the leadership of the foundation's chairman, Fred W. Smith, that brought this wonderful resolution to a patriotic emergency. When I described the circumstances as "providential," Sidney Hart, a scholar on the Portrait Gallery staff, told me that this was one of Washington's favorite words.

It means something, I believe, that this great image of George Washington was saved by a region of the country that did not even exist as part of the United States during his term of office and might, in fact, have been saved by a community of Americans of Asian origin who became citizens centuries after his death. With the display of this portrait, we celebrate Washington's role in history, of course, but more than that, his effect on our own lives today, on the nation, and on the system we have all inherited. It is a precious legacy.

And none of it must ever be taken for granted.

Marc Pachter
Director, National Portrait Gallery

★ *A Letter from the Donald W. Reynolds Foundation*

I T SEEMS ONLY APPROPRIATE THAT A FOUNDATION FUNDED BY a media magnate would learn about the potential "loss" of the Lansdowne portrait of George Washington through a newspaper article in the *Wall Street Journal*. That, in fact, is how the saga to save the painting began at the Las Vegas headquarters of the Donald W. Reynolds Foundation. An incredible set of circumstances aligned to make possible the purchase of the painting, funding for a permanent gallery space at the National Portrait Gallery, and a first-ever national tour of Stuart's icon of American history.

The opportunity and responsibility to "save George Washington for the American people" seemed the appropriate patriotic response for the foundation founded by a decorated World War II veteran who served his country bravely in Europe and the Pacific. Donald W. Reynolds cherished the freedom to express his entrepreneurial spirit and the opportunity to build a media empire from humble beginnings.

In addition to saving the painting, it was also the vision of our chairman, Fred W. Smith, to make the painting available for schoolchildren across the country to view. Again, a unique circumstance–the closing of the National Portrait Gallery building for renovation–made the national tour possible. The staff of the Gallery has done a remarkable job of taking that initial concept and developing a tour that will reintroduce Americans to our forgotten forefather–George Washington.

Reference to George Washington has almost vanished in classrooms and American history textbooks. For years Washington's portrait was displayed in every classroom. Today, that image has virtually disappeared. A major goal of the tour will be to reverse that trend. Copies of the painting will be made available to classrooms across America, and schoolchildren across the country will be given the opportunity to see the painting firsthand.

We believe that the leadership qualities that George Washington exhibited are the same leadership qualities that Americans are searching for today. The trustees of the Donald W. Reynolds Foundation are pleased and proud to be a part of this historic event.

Steven L. Anderson
President, Donald W. Reynolds Foundation

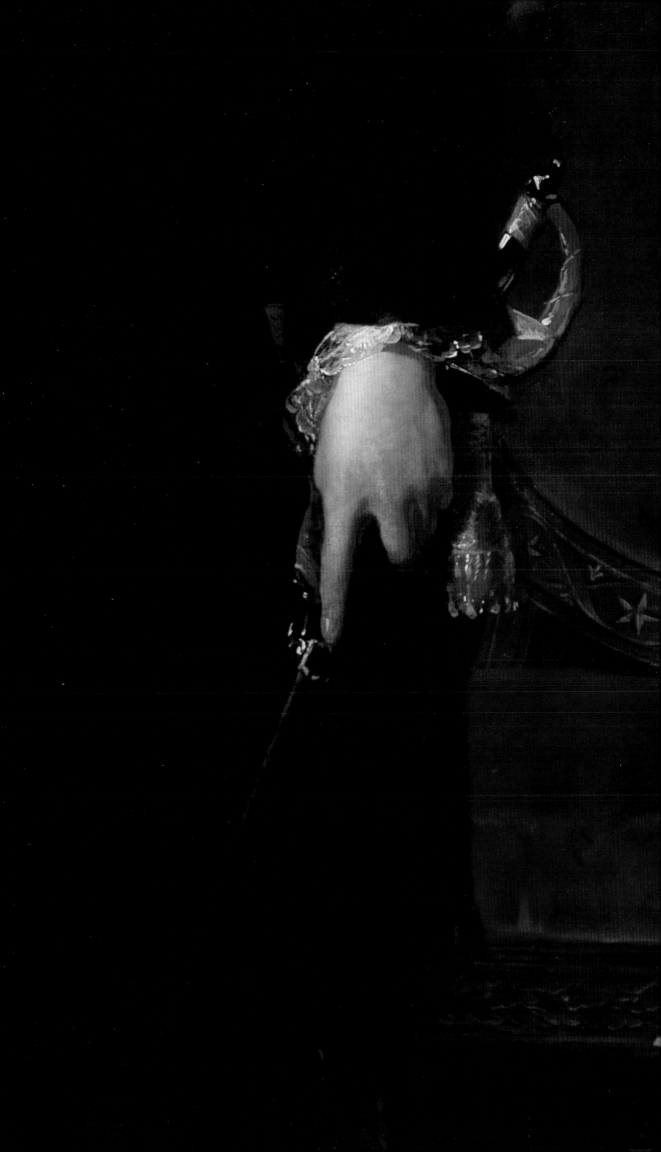

★ *George Washington: A National Treasure*

RICHARD BROOKHISER

IN TIMES OF CRISIS, ART CAN SEEM REMOTE, ESPECIALLY ART THAT commemorates the distant dead. Yet trouble was not invented for us; the dead waded through their share of it, and great artists can tell their story. Even the heroic portrait–traditionally an expression of triumph and contentment–can show us, if the artist was insightful and the subject was worthy, how a great man fought his way to the seeming calm of a plateau. What we need to bring to the task are our eyes, and our own experience.

When Gilbert Stuart came to paint President Washington in April 1796, he was not taking on a mysterious subject. George Washington had been the most famous man in America (and one of the most famous in the world) since 1775. Every American painter of note–and many of no note–had captured him. Cruder images, accurate or fanciful, decorated American almanacs and newspapers. A visitor from Russia, the land of icons, noted that "every American considers it his sacred duty" to have a Washington portrait on display in his home, "just as we have images of God's saints."

An unusually high number of Americans had seen the hero in the flesh. Most of the signage on "Ye Olde" buildings in the eastern United States boasting that "Washington slept here" is probably accurate: during the Revolution, he fought in five states, while as President, he made a point of visiting the states he had missed. People who missed his travels traveled to see him: in his brief intervals of retirement, hordes of callers descended on Mount Vernon–friends, strangers, and uninvited gawkers.

Most Americans knew his face; every American knew what he had done–he was first in war, and first in peace. In 1775 he had been chosen to command the

Continental army. Although he lost as many battles as he won, his victories–Trenton, Princeton, Monmouth (nominally a draw, but in fact a win), and Yorktown–were decisive. While winning the war, he kept his long-suffering troops obedient to civilian power. In 1787 he presided over the meeting–half political caucus, half theoretical seminar–that produced the Constitution, and his prestige was the greatest argument in favor of its adoption. "Be assured," wrote James Monroe, who opposed ratification, "his influence carried this government." In 1789 he was elected first President, and reelected four years later, both times unanimously. His administration began as a triumphal procession–en route to his first inauguration, in New York, he passed through Philadelphia, where 20,000 people came out to see him, out of a population of 28,000–but like every succeeding President, he had to make hard choices. The new country was almost bankrupt, and months into his first term the Bastille fell, inaugurating a quarter century of ideologically envenomed world war. By 1796 he had steered the United States through bitter disputes over the policies he had chosen to address these crises. A whiskey tax designed to raise badly needed revenue provoked a revolt on the frontier, while Jay's Treaty adjusting our postwar relations with Britain caused near-riots in New York and Philadelphia. But both Washington's tax policies and his peace policies worked, and his reputation, and the country, emerged from the strife as secure as ever. Washington was a celebrity, and he had earned his fame, not by playing basketball or a guitar, but by leading men and upholding the laws.

We still recognize Washington's face, thanks in part to Stuart, one of whose images decorates the dollar bill. That Stuart portrait is lodged in the pantheon of the national psyche, along with Honest Abe, Grant Wood's *American Gothic*, and the Thanksgiving turkey. But the achievements of the aged, tight-lipped man that Stuart shows us have grown dim in our minds. We know Washington was important, but we are not sure we know why. In becoming an icon, Washington has acquired the off-putting features of one: he strikes us as flat, impenetrable, and silent.

In the full-length "Lansdowne" portrait, however, Gilbert Stuart has left us a number of clues, some vivid, some subtle, to Washington's career and character– hints about the man who made such an impression on his contemporaries. If we listen to these hints, Washington can speak to us.

Washington, a delegate from Virginia to the Continental Congress, arrived in Philadelphia in his old uniform to show his willingness to fight.

———

George Washington by Charles Willson Peale, oil on canvas, 1772.
Washington-Custis-Lee Collection, Washington and Lee University, Lexington, Virginia

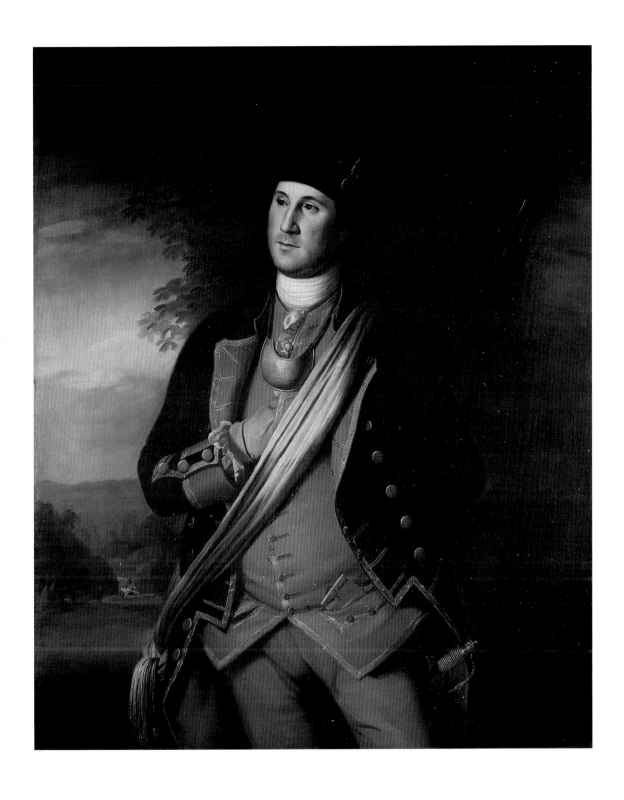

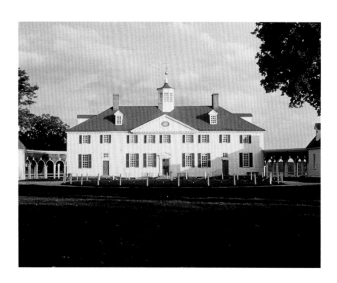

A modern view of the west facade of Mount Vernon, George Washington's home.

Courtesy of the Mount Vernon Ladies' Association, Virginia

During Washington's presidency and after his death, his face could be seen in many books, magazines, and almanacs. Engravings such as this one were available for framing and hanging.

George Washington by Cornelius Tiebout, after Gilbert Stuart Stipple engraving, 1800 National Portrait Gallery, Smithsonian Institution

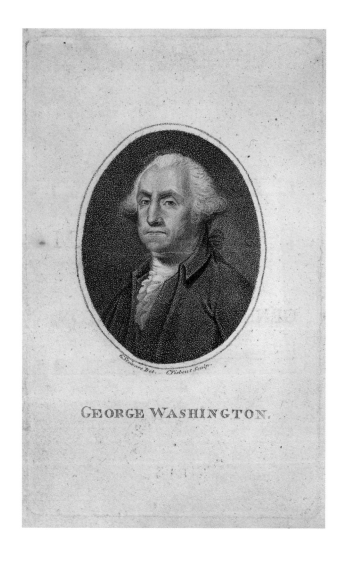

GEORGE WASHINGTON.

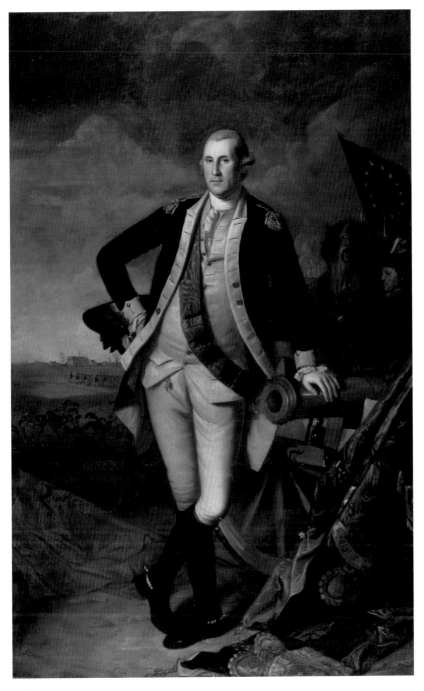

Washington was chosen as commander in chief of the Continental army, to fight the British during the American Revolution. The Battle of Princeton was a much-needed victory after a series of defeats.

Washington at the Battle of Princeton
by Charles Willson Peale
Oil on canvas, 1779
The Pennsylvania Academy
of the Fine Arts, Philadelphia;
gift of Maria McKean Allen
and Phebe Warren Downes

★   The first clue is the dress sword hanging at Washington's left hip (see page 12). By 1796, it had become an article of formal attire for him. But swords and fighting had been a central feature of his life, and his fame.

Washington was born in 1732 in Virginia, on the fringes of the British empire, third son of an ambitious planter. When George was eight years old, his twenty-two-year-old half-brother Lawrence was commissioned as a captain in the British army, to fight in one of the mother country's imperial wars against Spain. Lawrence later named the family estate after his commander, Admiral Edward Vernon; his blazing uniform must have made an impression on his younger sibling. In 1753, Lawrence's rich and powerful in-laws, the Fairfaxes, got George a commission in the Virginia militia; this time the enemy was France. Young Washington fought with enthusiasm. "I heard the bullet's whistle," he wrote after his first engagement, "and, believe me, there is something charming in the sound." When this comment was printed in a London newspaper, King George II commented that the Virginian fire-eater "would not think so if he had been used to hear many."

Washington heard the whistle of many bullets in his early twenties; many of them found their marks in the bodies of his comrades, for two of his battles were resounding British defeats. But he conducted himself with courage and energy. Two decades and another war later, when the Continental Congress was considering drastic measures against Britain, the mother country turned oppressor, the forty-three-year-old Washington, now a delegate from Virginia, arrived in Philadelphia in his old uniform to show his willingness to fight. His past military record made him the obvious choice for the American commander in chief.

When he accepted the post, he told Congress he did not think he was "equal" to the honor of his command. This was not mere modesty. In his twenties he had commanded small units and local theaters, and held a staff position. Now he had to master grand strategy and logistics, while facing the finest professional army and navy in the world, over a field of operations that stretched from Savannah to Quebec. His bravery did not fail him. At the Battle of Princeton he led an infantry charge on horseback; at the siege of Yorktown, when an aide cautioned him that they were exposed to enemy fire where they stood, he said, "If you think so, you are at liberty to step back." He learned early on that he needed well-trained troops–it is a myth that the Revolution was won by skirmishers fighting Indian style–and with the help of Baron von Steuben, the eccentric German professional soldier, and his own tireless attention to detail, he trained them. Finally, he grasped the strategic importance of American geography, especially rivers. Many of his most important moves were feints and maneuvers in which no shot was fired, undertaken to prevent the British from slicing up the Hudson River and cutting the rebellious colonies in half. The British military historian John Keegan thinks that four men mastered the significance of space, time, and terrain in North American warfare: Samuel Champlain, Ulysses Grant, Benedict Arnold, and

Washington. Fortunately, Washington understood the environment of war even better than Arnold.

An equally important aspect of Washington's military experience was the hold his leadership had on his men. We get a sense of this today from the accounts of common soldiers, sometimes written years after the fact. Well into the nineteenth century, one old man recalled his experiences as a teenager in a Rhode Island unit that had fought in the Battle of Trenton. Washington's post-Christmas surprise attack had been a splendid and desperately needed victory, but he knew the British would quickly retake the town. He posted his army outside Trenton, across a stream, leaving a garrison behind with orders to make a fighting retreat when the enemy arrived. The enemy came at dusk, and an artillery duel between the advancing British and Henry Knox's cannons began.

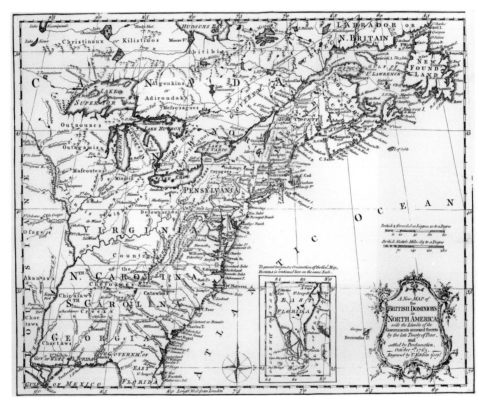

Washington's grasp of the strategic importance of American geography, especially its rivers, helped him maneuver against British troops.

A New Map of the British Dominions in North America
by Thomas Kitchin
Engraving, 1763
Library of Congress,
Washington, D.C.

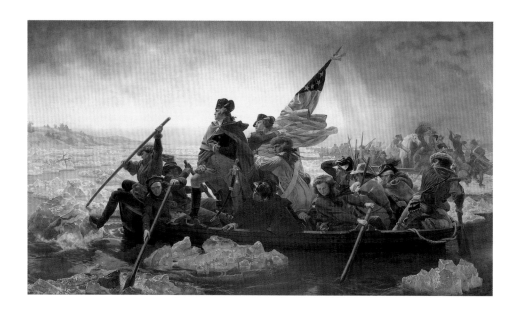

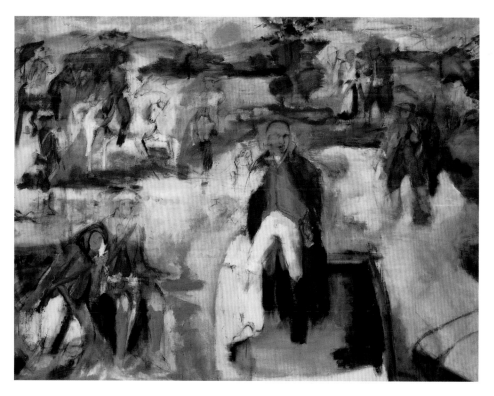

Many artists have portrayed Washington's crossing of the Delaware River to engage the British at Trenton, New Jersey. These are two interpretations, one from the nineteenth century and one from the twentieth.

Washington Crossing the Delaware by Emanuel Gottlieb Leutze, oil on canvas, 1851
The Metropolitan Museum of Art, New York City; gift of John Stewart Kennedy, 1897

Washington Crossing the Delaware by Larry Rivers, oil, graphite, and charcoal on linen, 1953
The Museum of Modern Art, New York City; given anonymously

The carnage of the Civil War, to say nothing of more recent wars, makes us think of the Revolution as a small-scale, even decorous affair. The number of deaths in Revolutionary battles was naturally limited by the logistics of supplying armies in the field; fewer men died when fewer men can be fed and armed. But those who were killed died as horribly as soldiers ever have. Artillery could be especially lethal. Cannon were loaded with grape–shells that exploded into shrapnel–or stuffed with chopped-up pieces of chain. These mini-missiles could dispatch men like buzz saws. The Rhode Islander remembered a panicky moment as the cannon fired. Only one narrow bridge led back over the stream to safety, and the retreating platoons crossing it were "crowded into a dense and solid mass." Ahead of him in the dim light he saw the mounted commander in chief survey-ing the retreat, and as he came to the end of the bridge, he was jostled against Washington's horse and boot. "The horse stood as firm as the rider, and seemed to understand that he was not to quit his post and station." This instant of physical contact made the young man understand something too: disorder was not chaos, darkness was not disaster; he must do what he should. Woody Allen has said that 85 percent of celebrity is just showing up. One hundred percent of leadership is showing up, in the right place, at the right time, and, if the leader fails, as he often does, showing up in the next place, and the next, until he succeeds.

As the war wound down in the spring of 1783, Washington had occasion to draw on the trust that his leadership instilled. Though the fighting had ended at Yorktown a year and a half earlier, the terms of peace were only just being settled. The officers of the army feared that when the war finally ended, Congress, broke as always, would send them home without pay. An anonymous address circulated through the army's last camp at Newburgh, New York, arguing that their only hope of influencing Congress was to appeal to it collectively, while they were still armed. The language was veiled, but the mutinous intent was clear. Washington defused it by calling a meeting of his sullen officers and recalling them to their duty. He ended his appeal with a gesture that has become famous: after proposing to read them a letter from a sympathetic congressman, he hesitated, then put on a pair of glasses. He begged his audience to excuse him: "I have grown grey in your service, and I find I am growing blind as well." The line produced conviction–and tears–because everyone in the room had experienced Washington's service and leadership in so many desperate moments. Any clever actor might have thought of Washington's gesture. But only a hero could have made it work.

★ The second clue to Washington's character that Stuart gives us is the remarkable highlighted face. This face tells us what the green and black engraving on the wrin-kled bills in our pockets can't–that Washington was a charismatic man. Charisma, which originally referred to the holy qualities of saints, now means the power to command men's attention and compel them to act. There are many forms of it:

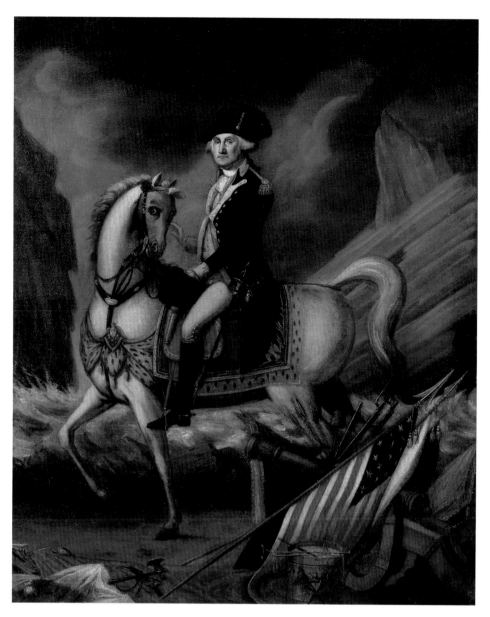

Washington's skill as a horseman served him well in war.

George Washington
by William Clark
Oil on canvas, 1800
On long-term loan to
the National Portrait Gallery,
Smithsonian Institution
from Eleanor M. Foster

orators, like Patrick Henry, can inspire; the clever, like Benjamin Franklin, can beguile. Washington, who had neither eloquence nor wit, impressed men through a combination of firmness and force that was partly physical, partly moral.

Standing six feet, three-and-one-half inches tall and showing the grace and muscle of a man who rode miles on horseback every day, Washington had one of the more impressive physiques of his time. When Abigail Adams first met him, she wrote a swooning letter to her husband John: "Mark his majestic fabric!" she quoted the poet Dryden, "he's a temple . . . built by hands divine." It must be said that Stuart fails to convey any sense of what Washington's body was like (though there are reasons why that failure is interesting, which we will get to). The rigid, black-clad form seems insubstantial, almost cartoonish. Stuart more than makes up for this lack, though, with the face.

The face radiates energy, without the slightest motion; it is solid as a rock, without seeming inert. Those blue eyes (a shade bluer than Washington's actually were) are both bright and hard; they might be diamond tips on a drill. And that clamped mouth with the curved lip expresses so much by repressing everything. No speech could be as forceful as what he is not saying.

What Washington isn't saying is quite possibly something angry. He had a terrible temper, and he waged a lifelong struggle to control it. When he was a teenager, Thomas, Lord Fairfax, the rich neighbor who employed Washington as a surveyor before placing him in the militia, wrote his mother that his only complaint about the young man was that he did not "govern . . . his temper." When he was in his sixties, Thomas Jefferson, Washington's former secretary of state, noted that at a cabinet meeting the old man "got into one of those passions where he cannot command himself." Stories of his displeasure fill the folklore of the founding. At a dicey moment during the Battle of Monmouth, one of Washington's generals heard him swearing "till the leaves shook on the trees. . . . Never have I enjoyed such swearing before or since. Sir, on that memorable day, he swore like an angel from heaven." At the Constitutional Convention, two young delegates, Alexander Hamilton and Gouverneur Morris, made a bet that Morris would not go up to Washington, slap him on the back, and compliment him on how well he looked. Morris won the bet, but said that the look Washington gave him after his hail-fellow greeting was the worst moment of his life. (Since Morris had burned the flesh off one of his arms in an accident and lost one of his legs in another, he had some experience with bad moments.) The problem with these stories is that they are not true: the general who claimed to have heard Washington's profanities at Monmouth was miles away from the commander in chief at the time, while the story about Morris and the bet exists in three contemporaneous but different versions, which suggests that it originated as a joke. But the reason both stories have been told and retold is that they capture a truth: Washington was a dangerous man. His self-control impressed people; so did the danger.

Gilbert Stuart figured in an authentic story of Washington's wrath. Stuart told Henry Lee, a Revolutionary War veteran, that his famous subject had a temper. Lee, who was a friend of the Washingtons', passed the comment on. Martha Washington resented the artist's impertinence. Lee added that Stuart had said the temper was under "wonderful control." George remarked, "Mr. Stuart is right."

The by-product of Washington's long wrestling with his anger was not exhaustion or paralysis, but a remarkable steadiness of purpose. His interior furnace was not allowed to flare away in random eruptions, but was banked for the long haul, the follow through. His public career demanded all of his capacity for steadfastness. The Revolution was our longest war, until Vietnam. Washington was in uniform for eight and a half years–longer than the Civil War and our participation in World War II combined. After five years off, he served two full back-to-back terms as President. Eleven other Presidents have repeated the feat, making it fairly common, but its frequency should not make us forget that almost every second term in American history has been weighed down by problems or outright disasters, from Monica to Iran-Contra to the British occupying Washington, D.C., and burning the White House. Washington's second term, with its fights over taxes and diplomacy, was no exception. The length and the stress of double presidencies weaken health and shorten lives; certainly Washington was an old sixty-four when Stuart met him. Together, Washington's service as commander in chief and President adds up to sixteen and a half years at the height of power and responsibility; Franklin Roosevelt's presidency, from his first inauguration to his death, lasted only twelve years.

In his old age, Thomas Jefferson, once a colleague of Washington's, later a critic, looked back on his marathoner's determination. Washington's mind "was slow in operation . . . but sure in conclusion," Jefferson wrote. "Perhaps the strongest feature in his character was prudence, never acting until every circumstance, every consideration, was maturely weighed; refraining if he saw a doubt, but, when once decided, going through with his purpose, whatever obstacles opposed." (The modernist poet William Carlos Williams would give Jefferson's thoughts a literary spin: "[Washington] had a will bred in the slow woods so that when he moved the world moved out of his way.")

Jefferson's tribute is a little left-handed, though. He does not quite say, though he clearly thinks, that he was smarter than his old boss, or at least quicker. No doubt the genius of Monticello was quicker on the uptake. What Washington knew, and what Jefferson only half-recognized, is that speed of analysis is not all. Take a good look at your problems; they will be with you for a long time. Only if you are equally tenacious will you solve them.

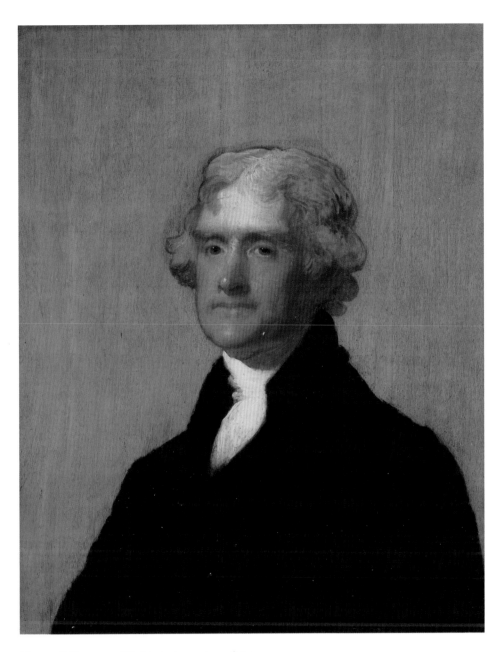

Thomas Jefferson was Washington's secretary of state.

Thomas Jefferson
by Gilbert Stuart
Oil on panel, 1805
National Portrait Gallery,
Smithsonian Institution, and Monticello,
Thomas Jefferson Memorial Foundation;
gift of the Regents of the Smithsonian Institution,
the Thomas Jefferson Memorial Foundation,
and the Enid and Crosby Kemper Foundation

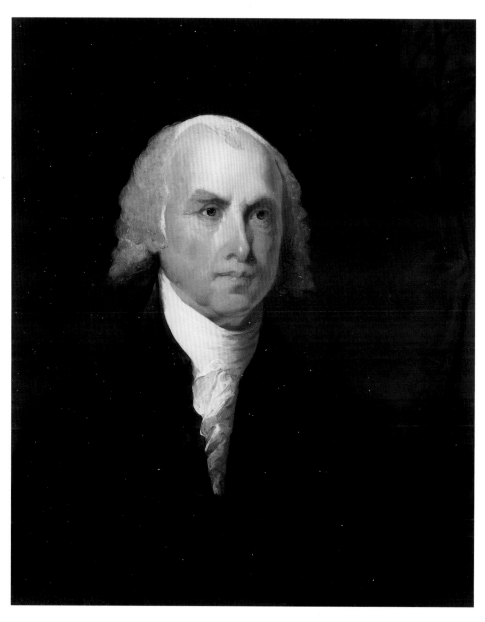

James Madison, Alexander Hamilton, and John Jay together wrote the Federalist Papers, promoting the ratification of the Constitution.

James Madison
by Gilbert Stuart
Oil on wood, circa 1821
National Gallery of Art,
Washington, D.C.;
Ailsa Mellon Bruce Fund

★   The third clue to Washington's character in Stuart's painting refers directly to the question of Washington's ability as a thinker. George's father probably intended to send his third son, as his first two had been sent, to England for what we now call secondary school. But he died when George was eleven, and the boy's schooling, such as it was, ended four or five years later. All his life Washington was embarrassed by his education, which he called "defective." Behind his back, some of his contemporaries agreed: John Adams, who was a graduate of Harvard, called him "unlearned" and "unread"; Aaron Burr, a Princeton man, claimed that he could not spell a simple sentence.

But whatever Washington and a few educated wiseacres thought, he had a powerful connection to ideas. Stuart symbolizes it with the books he places on and underneath his table (see page 76). One of the volumes on the floor is labeled *Constitution & Laws of the United States*; another on the tabletop is labeled *Federalist*.

The Constitution and the Federalist Papers are, with the Declaration of Independence, two of the three most important documents of the founding, and Washington was linked to both. The delegates to the Constitutional Convention had chosen him, by a unanimous vote, to preside. Though he said little (speaking briefly only three times), his presence at the convention gave it a seal of approval. The existing constitution, the Articles of Confederation, stipulated that all thirteen states must approve any change to the fundamental laws. But Rhode Island refused to send delegates to the convention, New Hampshire's came late, and most of New York's left early, in disgust with the reforming tendency of the meeting. Powerful men in key states, such as Patrick Henry in Virginia and Sam Adams in Massachusetts, viewed the convention with suspicion, fearing it as a virtual coup by a faction of ambitious nationalists. Yet Washington, as commander in chief, had held more power than anyone in America, and he had given it up. If he participated in the convention and approved its handiwork, then it could not be a power grab.

The essays that make up the Federalist Papers, now read as an oracle of constitutional interpretation, were dashed off by Alexander Hamilton, James Madison, and John Jay as pro-ratification polemics in New York newspapers. Washington had them reprinted in Richmond, to influence the ratification debate in Virginia. But this was not his only tie to the authors, or their thoughts. He had corresponded with them before the convention met, soliciting their suggestions for change. (Hamilton had been an officer on his staff; Madison was a fellow Virginian.) After the Constitution went into effect, President Washington appointed Hamilton treasury secretary and Jay chief justice, while Representative Madison served as an informal adviser and speechwriter.

Men of ideas clustered around Washington because he was the preeminent leader whose approval was necessary to give any idea a chance. Washington reached out to men of ideas because he knew he needed to draw on the country's best minds. There were times when the brain power around him was incandescent. In his first term as President, when he had to deliver his third annual message to Congress, he took suggestions from Madison and Jefferson (his secretary of state), gave them to Hamilton to work up, then sent the draft to Madison to rewrite. How many other Presidents have had such advisers? How many would have had the confidence to turn to them if they had been available? But Washington had to go beyond taking good advice. Since his brilliant contemporaries often disagreed–Jefferson finally concluded that Hamilton was a monarchist and a British toady, while Hamilton called Jefferson a "contemptible hypocrite"–he had to choose among them. Washington is the classic example of a leader who is not an intellectual himself, but who knows that he must understand the best ideas of the day and judge among them.

His judgment was vital, because there were many ideas available in the world for leaders to choose from. Eighteenth-century rulers collected ideas and thinkers, just as they collected paintings and palaces. Frederick the Great invited Voltaire to visit his court; Catherine the Great brought Diderot to hers. As a boy, George III had studied Viscount Bolingbroke's *The Idea of a Patriot King*, one of the most popular political essays of the day; when he became a king himself, he had intelligent literary conversations with Samuel Johnson and James Boswell. But all the ideas these rulers dabbled in fortified them in their desire to wield power. (They would wield it for the good, of course, but it would never leave their enlightened hands.) Washington studied at a different school. The ideas that he heard debated in the Continental Congress and at the Philadelphia Convention, and that he took from his brilliant colleagues, all shared the premise that no man, however enlightened, ruled by hereditary right or for life. Good intentions did not sanctify absolute power; the final service of a good ruler was to give his power up.

★   The fourth clue in our painting is conveyed by Washington's dress and demeanor. He wears a long black velvet suit, with lace frill on his shirt. No one today dresses like this (although some designers in London and Milan dress their male models in velvet, or three-quarter-length coats). Yet Washington's dress is not as remote from ours as it might seem at first glance. He is not wearing armor, or plumes, or jeweled insignia; his black and white are the colors of modern formal wear. His posture suggests reserve. This was true to life. Washington met more of his fellow Americans than any other American, but he was never familiar. The joke about Gouverneur Morris and the bet depends on Washington's sense of himself and of his personal space. Together, the look and the stance of Stuart's portrait define a role: Washington was a gentleman.

Today, when every head of government in the western world except the pope dresses as if he or she could slip into a board meeting, if not a wedding party, we must remind ourselves what an innovation a gentleman in power was. Most of the rulers of the world were kings and queens, and their ermines, leopard skins, and diamonds from the mines of India can be studied in the paintings in any large museum. So can the commanding cock of their heads and the sweep of their sceptered arms.

The thrones of the world were about to totter; the American Revolution was the first indirect blow to their foundations. But the way of the gentleman was not the only option that a new generation of revolutionaries could take. France's revolution, which came soon on the heels of ours, was begun by liberal-minded aristocrats (the Marquis de Lafayette sent Washington a key to the Bastille). Leadership soon passed, however, to the Parisian mobs, who called themselves *sans-culottes*, spurning genteel silken knickers in favor of their honest plebeian trousers. In the early nineteenth century, Lord Byron, fighting in the Greek war of independence, went exotic, adopting Balkan bandit gear. Other revolutionaries behaved more grandly than the monarchs they overthrew, even as they amassed more power than their predecessors. After Napoleon Bonaparte crowned himself Emperor of France, he aped the regalia of Charlemagne and Byzantium; his image, in some of his late portraits, is as bedizened as the Las Vegas Elvis.

Personal style can symbolize political style. Compared to the courtliness of the past, and to the brutal or self-aggrandizing fashions that would follow, the black coat and dignified manner of Stuart's Washington represent a decorous middle way. He had not adopted it by accident; the externals of dress and behavior were never far from Washington's mind.

Five weeks before his first inauguration, he sent a letter of advice to a nephew, George Steptoe Washington. (Childless himself, Washington had to direct his paternal feelings to nieces and nephews, stepchildren, and certain young colleagues, like Morris and Lafayette.) "You have now arrived to that age when you must quit the trifling amusements of a boy," uncle Washington wrote, "and assume the more dignified manners of a man." What did the older George tell the younger one? He urged his nephew to acquire "knowledge" and "the habit of industry." He told him to seek "good company," so as to "improv[e] your manners." He was very particular about "the article of clothing," instructing the young man to balance "decency," "cleanliness," and "frugality." "You should always keep some clothes to wear to Church, or on particular occasions, which should not be worn everyday . . . whenever it is necessary to get new clothes, those which have been kept for particular occasions will then come in [handy] as every-day ones."

At the end of his letter, Washington mentioned "the moral virtues"–a perennial theme of advice to the young. After his death, Washington himself would become a figure of moral instruction. The stories that his first biographer, Mason Locke Weems, made up and made famous–Washington and the cherry tree; Washington's father planting a garden so that the seedlings came up spelling his son's name–all had moral points. The story of the cherry tree inculcated honesty in children and wise discipline in parents. (Beating children for every offense turns them into liars; because Washington's father behaved differently, so did George.)

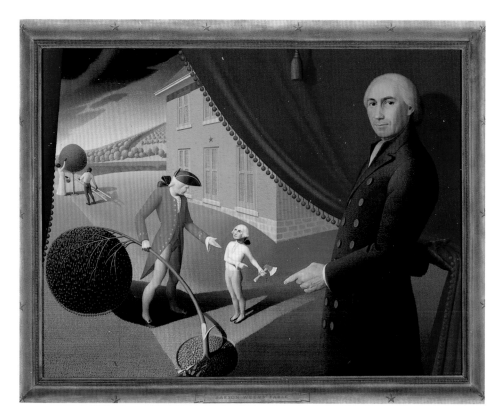

Mason Locke "Parson" Weems deliberately wrote fictional stories about Washington's life–including the story about Washington chopping down a cherry tree–so that he could present the former President as a role model for children.

Parson Weems' Fable
by Grant Wood
Oil on canvas, 1939
Amon Carter Museum,
Fort Worth, Texas

The story of the seedlings taught the divine ordering of the universe: even as George's name did not spring up by accident, so he, and we, are placed on earth by a Creator. Thus Parson Weems. The historical Washington, however, instructing his nephew, only writes that the moral virtues "may, perhaps, more properly be the subject of a future letter."

This rather large omission also characterized a set of instructions that Washington copied carefully into a notebook when he was a teenager: *The Rules of Civility & Decent Behaviour in Company and Conversation.* (Washington's copy is in the Library of Congress.) This list of 110 rules is a version of a set originally compiled by sixteenth-century French Jesuits. When young Washington wrote them down in colonial Virginia in the mid-1740s, he was eager to make his way in the world; such rules must have struck him, and the adult who gave them to him, as a useful guide. And guide they do, often exhaustively: "In pulling off your hat to persons of distinction, [such] as noblemen, justices, churchmen, &c., make a reverence, bowing more or less according to the custom of the better bred, and quality of the persons. Among your equals expect not always that they should begin with you first, but to pull off the hat when there is no need is affectation" (Rule #26). Yet there is precious little explicit moral instruction in the *Rules.* A reminder of the First and Fifth Commandments (#108), a veiled warning against whoring (#109), and an exhortation to "keep alive in your breast that little spark of celestial fire called conscience" (#110) are about it, and they are very late in coming.

Instead, the *Rules* are concerned with etiquette—how to walk, talk, dress, and eat. These are the externals of life, and they can strike us as superficial. Yet the Jesuits who wrote the *Rules* knew something, which the distant student who copied them learned: externals have a way of working inwards. The *Rules* are exercises in attention. In order to decide when properly to take off your hat, you must first be aware that there are others about you whom you should salute, or who may be saluting you. This awareness of our social environment is necessary in dozens of situations in life, from the dinner table ("Drink not nor talk with your mouth full"—Rule #98) to the fireplace ("Spit not into the fire . . . especially if there be meat before it"—Rule #9). Whenever we drink, talk, or spit we have to be mindful of those around us, whether they are friends or strangers, because they, like us, have sensibilities that deserve respect. Civility, it turns out, is an external practice of virtue.

For Washington it was not merely a virtue of private life. The thousands of people he met, as commander in chief and President, covered a huge variety of types—Virginia planters, New England farmers, violent frontiersman, pacifist Quakers. The former Indian fighter had to deal with Indian allies; the slave owner had to command free black soldiers. Congressmen who frustrated him, foreign diplomats who wished to patronize or manipulate him, all came his way. These encounters were eased by a practice of civility that had become second nature to him. Politeness, in Washington's career, was a form of politics.

★   Stuart's painting shows no slaves, though there were many in Washington's life. At the time Stuart painted him, about three hundred lived at Mount Vernon. Many men of the eighteenth century ignored the moral issue of slavery, and most of those who did not were unable or unwilling to face it squarely. We have no choice.

At the end of his life, Washington concluded that he had no choice either. By 1796, he had already devised a plan to divide his estate into four pieces, and rent them out to English farmers, who would be able to hire his freed slaves as agricultural laborers. He confided to his secretary, Tobias Lear, that one of the benefits of the scheme would be "to liberate a certain species of property which I possess very repugnantly to my own feelings." (Like many Americans of the day, he avoided the word "slave," partly because he did not wish to discuss the facts plainly, partly because he believed that speaking of slavery as if it were a matter of course would give it a tacit moral recognition it should not have.) Washington's plan came to nothing; no one wanted to rent Mount Vernon's exhausted soil.

He finally addressed slavery in one of the last political acts of his life. In his last will and testament, written in July 1799, Washington directed that all his slaves be freed at the death of his wife. He set aside enough money to support those too old or too young to work; most important, he asked that the young be taught to read, write and practice "some useful occupation." He did not dispatch them over the Ohio to free territory, or across the Atlantic to some such place as Liberia. He wanted to prepare them to live in the world in which they had grown up. Some idealistic slave owners of the founding generation freed their slaves in their wills, but the notion of educating soon-to-be-liberated slaves was so radical that at the beginning of the nineteenth century, Virginia banned the practice. All his slaves were, however, freed as he had stipulated. Washington died in December 1799, and Martha decided to liberate them a year later. The estate paid pensions to former slaves who wanted them until 1833.

The act of freeing his slaves called upon every trait suggested in Stuart's painting. Washington was guided by the ideas that all his revolutionary colleagues shared. (Jefferson, a fellow slaveholder, wrote that "All men are created equal"; Hamilton, an immigrant from the island slave factories of the Caribbean, helped begin the process of abolition in New York.) Washington's determination impelled him, at the end of his life, to do the right thing. Civility and wartime memories joined in his treatment of one slave, William Lee ("my Mulatto man William"), who had been his personal servant during the Revolution. Lee, himself a fine horseman, had accompanied Washington in fox hunts and battles. Drink and injuries slowed

Washington copied out the Rules of Civility and Decent Behaviour in Company and Conversation *in about 1744, as a guide to behavior.*

Library of Congress, Washington, D.C.

Rules of Civility & Decent Behaviour
In Company and Conversation

1 Every Action done in Company, ought to be with Some Sign of Respect, to those that are present.

2 When in Company, put not your Hands to any Part of the Body, not usualy Discovered.

3 Shew Nothing to your freind that may affright him.

4 In the Presence of Others Sing not to yourself with a humming Noise, nor Drum with your Fingers or Feet.

5 If You Cough, Sneeze, Sigh, or Yawn, do it not Loud but Privately; and Speak not in your Yawning, but put Your handkerchief or Hand before your face and turn aside.

6 Sleep not when others Speak, Sit not when others stand, Speak not when you Should hold your Peace, walk not on when others Stop.

7 Put not off your Cloths in the presence of Others, nor go out your Chamber half Drest.

8 At Play and at Fire its Good manners to Give Place to the last Commer, and affect not to Speak Louder than Ordinary.

9 Spit not in the Fire, nor Stoop low before it neither Put your Hands into the Flames to warm them, nor Set your Feet upon the Fire especially if there be meat before it.

10 When you Sit down, Keep your Feet firm and Even; without putting one on the other or Crossing them.

11 Shift not yourself in the Sight of others nor Gnaw your nails.

12 Shake not the head, Feet, or Legs rowl not the Eys lift not one eyebrow higher than the other wry not the mouth, and bedew no mans face with your Spittle, by approaching too near him when you Speak.

George Washington: A National Treasure | 33

him down as an old man, but he always asked to see veterans who visited Mount Vernon; he would reminisce with them about the war. "Was it not cold enough at Valley Forge? Yes, was it; and I am sure you remember it was hot enough at Monmouth." William Lee is the second person mentioned in Washington's will, after Martha, and he is given his immediate freedom, if he should wish it, "as a testimony of my sense of his attachment to me, and for his faithful services during the Revolutionary War."

We wish Washington had done more; we always want our fathers, real and symbolic, to fix our problems for us. Washington, at the end of his life, did more than any other slaveholding President, including Jefferson and Madison.

★   One last question remains, before we leave Washington and Stuart's portrait. What exactly is he doing?

There is a tradition that he is speaking, perhaps delivering his Farewell Address. This address—the only presidential speech read every year in the Senate—was already on his mind when he sat for Stuart. Washington had asked Madison to draft a farewell in 1792, when he contemplated stepping down after his first term. (Madison, and all Washington's by-then squabbling advisers, united in beseeching him to stay on.) By the spring of 1796, he had definitely decided not to run for President a third time, and he sent his own draft of a farewell, incorporating Madison's work, to Hamilton, who then produced a new version. With tight editing by Washington, this became the text that was released to the country in September 1796. (Washington had also asked John Jay for his comments; he thus brought together the three authors of the Federalist Papers for their last collaboration.) The Farewell Address urged Americans to stay united, and to pursue the national interest in foreign affairs. The news hook, however, was Washington's announcement of his intention to return to private life.

The idea that Stuart has painted this moment is a pretty story, but false. Washington never spoke the Farewell Address, but had it printed in a Philadelphia newspaper. Nor was speechifying among his gifts. For Stuart to have depicted him orating would have been a blunder, like showing the pacific Jefferson in uniform, or the worldly Franklin in a pulpit.

Washington was, however, a theatrical man. He loved plays all his life, and he knew the value of dramatic action, whether it was sitting on a horse by a bridge full of fearful boys, or putting on his reading glasses before an audience of angry men. The setting in which Stuart has placed him, despite the table and books, is surely no office. The columns and the open spaces, however much they quote the conventional props of public life in eighteenth-century paintings, also make it look very much like an outdoor stage—a classical amphitheater, perhaps. Washington is making a gesture.

He points in front of him and outside the frame of the painting, to our left. Evidently there has been a storm, because behind his head, to the right, we can

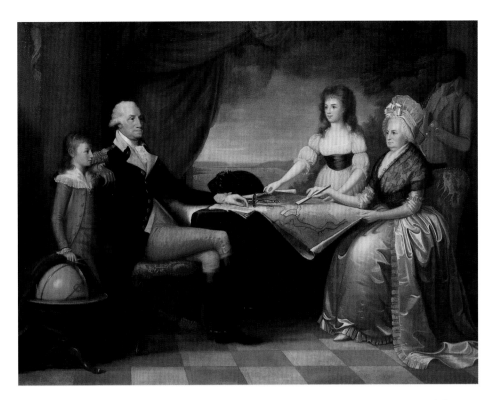

Washington's personal servant, the slave William Lee, appears to the far right in this image of the Washington family.

The Washington Family
by Edward Savage
Oil on canvas, 1789–1796
National Gallery of Art,
Washington, D.C.;
Andrew W. Mellon Collection

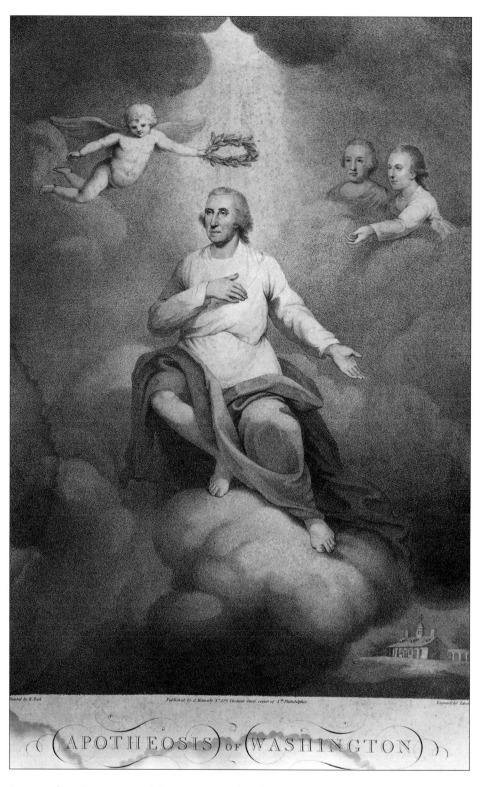

Images such as this one captured the intense sense of grief that Americans felt upon Washington's death in 1799.

Apotheosis of Washington
by David Edwin after Rembrandt Peale
Stipple engraving, circa 1800
National Portrait Gallery, Smithsonian Institution

see a rainbow (its bars of color are picked up in the stripes of the seal of the United States on the back of his chair). The rainbow is behind him, but the light comes from in front of him. He is pointing to the future.

He himself, however, is about to retire. Washington, the most discreet of men, told no one besides his collaborators about his Farewell Address, but by 1796 he felt himself to be an old man (he had already lived fourteen years longer than his father). A portraitist as intuitive as Stuart would have picked this up.

This is why the awkward unphysicality, so unlike Washington the leader, makes sense. He is preparing to leave the stage. His body has already gone; the forceful head will soon follow. The black of his velvet suit is not just gentlemanly; it is funereal. The chair behind him, in which he will evidently sit once the gesture is completed, is an upright forerunner of the grave.

Retirement was not an accidental ending to George Washington's career; it was an integral part of his life's plan. In June 1788, as the Constitution hung in the balance of the state ratifying conventions, he wrote Lafayette that the United States should show the world that "Mankind" was not "made for a master." He had refused to be that master, and he had rebuked anyone–including his own beloved officers– who thought of imposing such terms. For more than twenty years, Washington had done every task that had come his way; the last task was to step aside, and return his authority to the people, and their descendants: to us.

The gesture says, "I am going; here you are."

★ *Chronology of George Washington's Life and Times*

FREDERICK S. VOSS

★ Items in italic are general historical items

1732   February 22 (February 11 Old Style): Born at Popes Creek, Virginia

1749   Appointed surveyor for Culpeper County, Virginia

1751   Contracts smallpox on a trip to the West Indies with his half-brother Lawrence; the disease leaves him scarred for life

1752   Appointed major in Virginia militia

1754   Lieutenant Colonel Washington subdues small French detachment in western Pennsylvania, an incident said to have sparked the French and Indian War. Washington is later defeated by the French at Fort Necessity

1755   Serves as aide-de-camp to British Major General Edward Braddock. French defeat this force at Fort Duquesne, Pennsylvania. Braddock killed in the battle; Washington widely praised for courage in the face of disaster

1756–58   Oversees defense of frontier as commander of Virginia's troops during French and Indian War

1758   Elected to Virginia House of Burgesses (colonial legislature)

1759   Marries Martha Dandridge Custis

1761   Inherits 2,000-acre Mount Vernon plantation, which he had rented since 1754. By the time of his death he expanded it to 8,000 acres, with more than 3,000 acres under cultivation

1765   *Parliament passes Stamp Act, imposing new taxes on American colonies*

1766–67   *Stamp Act repealed. Parliament enacts Townshend duties on various goods shipped to colonies*

1769   Becomes a leader of Virginia's protest against Townshend duties in House of Burgesses

1773   *Bostonians dump tea from a merchant ship overboard to protest tea tax. Subsequently, Parliament enacts so-called Intolerable Acts against Boston*

1774   *First Continental Congress convened to protest the heavy handedness of British rule*

    Represents Virginia in Continental Congress

1775   *War for Independence begins at Lexington and Concord, Massachusetts*

    Second Continental Congress unanimously appoints Washington commander-in-chief of newly formed Continental army

    George III declares Washington and all other participants in the rebellion traitors

1776	*Continental Congress approves Declaration of Independence; first printed copies issued July 4, 1776*
	August: Defeated at Battle of Long Island
	November: Forced to retreat into New Jersey after British forces occupy New York City
	December: Crosses Delaware River to defeat British at Trenton
1777	Defeated at battles of Brandywine and Germantown
	October: American forces under Horatio Gates claim major triumph at Battle of Saratoga, a turning point of the war
	December: Washington's army camps for the winter at Valley Forge, outside of British-occupied Philadelphia
1778	June: Defeats British at the Battle of Monmouth
	U.S. gains an ally in France; British attempt at reconciliation with Americans fails
1781	October: Washington's army, with French support, defeats British at Battle of Yorktown, ending military phase of War for Independence
1783	*Treaty of Paris, making peace between Britain and former American colonies, signed*
	Resigns commander-in-chief's commission
1786	*Annapolis convention of delegates from five states calls for Constitutional Convention to consider altering the Articles of Confederation, which had governed the country since 1777*
1787	Serves as presiding officer of Constitutional Convention in Philadelphia; his support for new Constitution becomes key factor in winning its approval from the requisite nine states
1789	Unanimously elected by Electoral College to serve as first President of the United States
	Executive departments of State, War, and Treasury are created, and Congress passes the Federal Judiciary Act, organizing the country's judicial system
1790	Signs legislation placing nation's capital on the Potomac River
1791	Signs act creating a national bank; establishes tradition of presidential cabinet meeting
1792	Exercises presidential veto for the first time
1793	Unanimously reelected to the presidency by Electoral College
	Issues Proclamation of Neutrality to avoid American involvement during hostilities between England and France; criticized for not being more sympathetic to the French

1794	Asserts primacy of federal authority by authorizing use of militia to suppress uprising over federal whiskey tax in western Pennsylvania
1795	Sends Jay Treaty–a negotiated agreement with Great Britain–to Senate for ratification. Treaty, regarded by many as a sellout to English interests, inspires some of fiercest press attacks ever made on Washington
1796	April: Sits for Gilbert Stuart's full-length Lansdowne painting, commissioned by Senator William Bingham of Philadelphia for the Marquis of Lansdowne
	Announces in Farewell Address his intention not to seek a third presidential term; warns against divisiveness of political party rivalries and hazards of permanent foreign alliances
1797	Retires to Mount Vernon
1799	Contracts throat infection while touring his plantation through rain and snow in the late fall. Dies on December 14, weakened by the purging and bleeding that were common treatments for such ailments
1800	Martha Washington frees Mount Vernon's slaves, according to the terms of George Washington's will
1806	Lansdowne painting sold to American merchant-banker Samuel Williams
1808	Parson Weems writes *The Life of George Washington*, which includes many fictional stories about Washington's life
1827	Lansdowne painting won by John Delaware Lewis in a lottery, after Williams's business fails; painting is passed down in the Lewis family
1876	Lansdowne painting lent to Philadelphia Centennial Exposition
1885	Washington Monument completed in Washington, D.C.
1889	Archibald Philip Primrose, fifth Earl of Rosebery, purchases Lansdowne painting; it is passed down in the family
1932	Two-hundredth anniversary of Washington's birth celebrated across United States; posters based on Stuart's Lansdowne image are sent to schools nationwide. Lansdowne portrait is lent to the George Washington Bicentennial Historical Loan Exhibition at the Corcoran Gallery of Art
1968	Lansdowne painting lent to opening of the National Portrait Gallery in Washington, D.C., where it remains on long-term loan until 2001
1976	As part of the bicentennial celebration, Congress promotes Washington to six-star General of the Armies so that he will rank above all other American generals
2001	National Portrait Gallery, Smithsonian Institution, purchases Lansdowne painting of George Washington for the nation

★ *The Story of the Lansdowne Washington*

MARGARET C. S. CHRISTMAN

THIS MONUMENTAL EIGHT-BY-FIVE-FOOT PORTRAIT OF PRESIDENT George Washington, posing in full grandeur as the republican head of state, was painted by Gilbert Stuart in 1796 and sent to England that same year, as a gift to the Marquis of Lansdowne from Senator and Mrs. William Bingham of Philadelphia. Therein lies a tale–the story of the fortuitous coming together, thanks to a woman of legendary charm and a man of exceptional enterprise, of the greatest man of the age with the premier portrait painter of his time and place. The initial outcome was a "magnificent compliment" for a nobleman who merited the gratitude of the young republic; the final outcome was a treasure for the American people.

The portrait hung until Lord Lansdowne's death in 1806 in the library of his London town house in Berkeley Square and afterward adorned the premises of Samuel Williams's "great American banking house" on Finsbury Square. It remained in private hands, incorporated into the collection of the fifth Earl of Rosebery in 1889, and it ultimately hung in a reconstructed seventeenth-century castle on the grounds of Dalmeny House in West Lothian, Scotland. In 1968, when America's National Portrait Gallery, established by act of Congress in 1962, was about to open its doors, the portrait arrived on loan and was installed in a place of honor, where it remained for thirty-two years. In 2001, when it was scheduled for auction unless the Gallery could come up with $20 million, the Donald W. Reynolds Foundation assured that the Portrait Gallery would have it always.

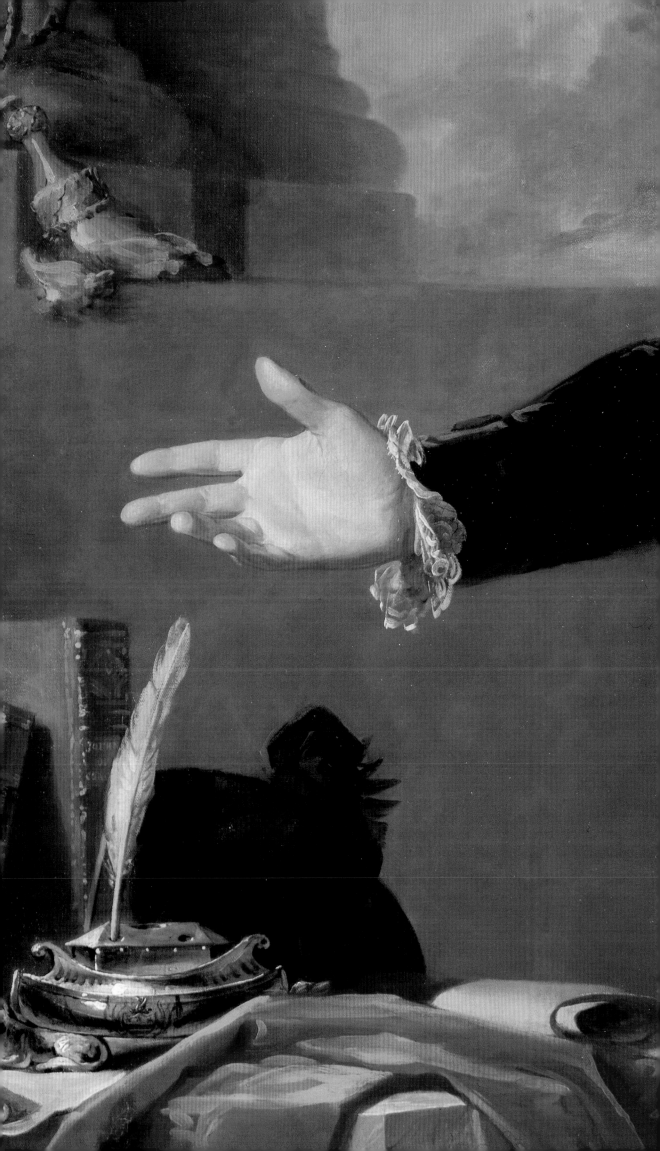

"I am under promise to Mrs. Bingham, to set for you tomorrow at nine oclock," wrote President George Washington to Gilbert Stuart on April 11, 1796, "and wishing to know if it be convenient to you that I should do so, and whether it shall be at your own house, (as she talked of the State House) I send this note to you, to ask information."

Washington as soldier and politician had been on the public stage for forty-five of his sixty-four years and had long since resigned himself to the necessity of accommodating artists. Agreeing to pose for a minor English painter, Robert Edge Pine, he wrote whimsically in 1785, "In for a penny, in for a pound, is an old adage. I am so hackneyed to the touches of the Painters pencil, that I am *now* altogether at their beck, and sit like patience on a Monument whilst they are delineating the lines of my face."

But the spring of 1796 was not a happy time for the President to pose for a portrait. Much to Washington's distress, differences in philosophy and policy espoused by Secretary of the Treasury Alexander Hamilton and Secretary of State Thomas Jefferson (allied with James Madison) had been brought to full-blown partisanship. Jeffersonian Republicans, in an affinity with the revolutionaries in France, took the side of that country in their war against England, an important American trading partner, and to the Federalists still in many ways the mother country. "We *think in English*," Alexander Hamilton remarked to the British minister.

But by 1794 the British government's outrageous violation of the rights of neutral ships on the high seas and its refusal to abide by the terms of the treaty that brought the American Revolution to a close was more than the country could tolerate. To avert a war, President Washington had dispatched Chief Justice John Jay to negotiate differences with the old enemy, and the resulting Treaty of Amity, Commerce, and Navigation had been ratified behind the closed doors of the Senate by a strict party line vote in June 1795. Leaked to the press, the Jay Treaty was denounced by the Republicans as a return to British domination and a repudiation of America's wartime alliance with France. "The cry against the Treaty," Washington told Alexander Hamilton, "is like that against a mad-dog." Protest meetings and effigy burnings erupted throughout the country. In Philadelphia a thousand-man mob paraded with the treaty on a stick, burned it in front of the residence of the English minister, and threw stones against the window of Federalist William Bingham's opulent mansion. At Charleston, John Rutledge, the President's nominee to succeed John Jay as chief justice, announced at a public meeting that "he had rather, the President should die, dearly as he loves him, than he should sign that treaty." But sign the treaty the President did on August 18, 1795.

Republicans in the House of Representatives, led by James Madison, were still determined to block the treaty by refusing to vote the appropriation necessary

One of the few references to Washington sitting for artist Gilbert Stuart is in this letter of April 11, 1796. Washington writes, "I am under promise to Mrs. Bingham, to set for you tomorrow at nine oclock."

The Earl of Rosebery

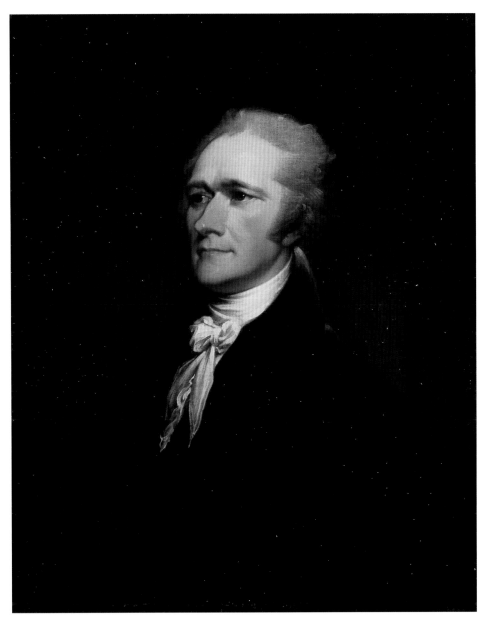

Secretary of the Treasury Alexander Hamilton returned to private life in January 1795, but continued to help and advise the President.

Alexander Hamilton
by John Trumbull
Oil on canvas, 1806
National Portrait Gallery,
Smithsonian Institution;
gift of Henry Cabot Lodge

for it to go into effect. A "long and animated discussion"–which Washington described as bringing "the Constitution, to the brink of a precipice" and putting "the peace happiness and prosperity of the Country into eminent danger"–began on April 7, 1796, "suspending, in a manner all other business; and agitating the public mind in a higher degree than it has been at any period since the Revolution." Not until April 30 did the public-relations campaign crying out for "Washington and Peace" carry the day. By a vote of 51 to 48, the motion allowing the treaty to go into effect was passed, and Madison wrote in disgust that the people had listened to the summons "to follow where Washington leads."

Enveloped in this atmosphere of passionate political conflict, the President prepared to keep his promise to Mrs. Bingham–even during this time when the old hero found himself the object of virulent personal attack in the Republican press. "We have given him the powers and prerogatives of a King," jeered newspaper editor Philip Freneau–"that rascal Freneau"–Washington called him. "He holds levees like a King, receives congratulations on his birthday like a King, makes treaties like a King, receives ambassadors like a King, answers petitions like a King, employs his old enemies like a King . . . swallows adulation like a King, and vomits offensive truths in your face."

These newspaper attacks, the thin-skinned Washington protested,

> unjust and unpleasant as they are, will occasion no change in my conduct; nor will they work any other effect in my mind, than to increase the anxious desire which has long possessed my breast, to enjoy in the shades of retirement the consolation of having rendered my Country every service my abilities were competent to, uninfluenced by pecuniary or ambitious considerations as they respected myself.

Such was Washington's frame of mind as he presented himself to Gilbert Stuart. He would insist to Henrietta Liston, the wife of the British minister, that "my countenance never yet betrayed my feelings"–a statement she disputed–but there could be no question that when the President posed for posterity, the obligation of upholding the honor and dignity of his office was an overriding consideration. We may say of Washington, John Adams reflected in 1811, "if he was not the greatest President, he was the best actor of presidency we have ever had."

Gilbert Stuart, the son of a Scottish-born millwright (also named Gilbert Stuart) and Elizabeth Anthony, daughter of a Rhode Island farmer, had from his teenage years exhibited an extraordinary talent for capturing a likeness. In 1775 he had gone to England and remained for five years with Benjamin West, mentor and teacher to three generations of American artists. West provided Stuart not so much with instruction in technique–Stuart saw things through his own eyes–but rather with an ambience that nourished his genius and provided an exposure to the world of culture and sophistication.

To contradict the critic who said he "made a tolerable likeness of a face, but as to the figure he could not get below the fifth button," Stuart painted the full-length *The Skater* (National Gallery of Art), which attracted attention at the Royal Academy exhibition in 1782. Shortly thereafter, Stuart "had his full share of the best business in London, and prices equal to any except Sir Joshua Reynolds, and Gainsborough." Assessed the *World* (London) in April 1787, "Stuart dives deep into *mind!* and brings up with him a conspicuous draught of character." Listed among the portraits "deserving of this great praise," was one of the Marquis of Lansdowne, a picture that has dropped from sight.

A mountain of debt, run up by extravagant living, prompted Stuart to move to Ireland in 1787. There he found a ready patronage that included commissions for several full-length portraits, notably John Fitzgibbon, Lord Chancellor of Ireland, attired in the full regalia of his office (Cleveland Museum of Art), and John Foster, Speaker of the Irish House of Commons, shown with gold mace and books alluding to his political career (see page 88).

Stuart fled Ireland–and his creditors–to return to America after an absence of eighteen years, telling his Irish chronicler, "There I expect to make a fortune by Washington alone." He landed in New York in 1793, and such was the hunger for the services of an accomplished artist that he lingered there for almost two years before proceeding to Philadelphia, the seat of government until 1800. On November 15, 1794, Mrs. John Jay reported that Stuart intended in ten days' time "to go to Philadelphia, to take a likeness of the President."

Provided with a letter of introduction from John Jay–who had posed for a portrait in England (with a replica ordered for his friend William Bingham) and for another likeness in New York–Stuart first met President Washington as he mingled with members of Congress and other gentlemen every Tuesday afternoon at three o'clock at his High (Market) Street residence. "Although accustomed to the first society in Europe, and possessed of great self-respect and excellent manner," Stuart, recorded his daughter Jane, "was so intimidated as to lose, for the moment all self-possession," but "he soon recovered himself, and entered into conversation, an art in which he was well versed."

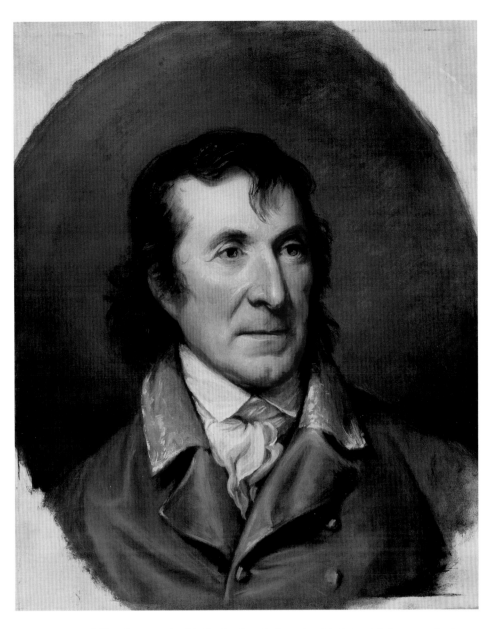

American artist Gilbert Stuart trained in England, and also painted in Ireland, before returning to the United States in 1793, where he hoped to make a fortune painting portraits of George Washington.

Gilbert Stuart
by Charles Willson Peale and Rembrandt Peale
Oil on canvas, 1805
The New-York Historical Society, New York City

Exactly when in 1795 Washington first sat for Gilbert Stuart is a matter of conflicting opinion, but the artist himself related it was "in ye winter season." On April 20, 1795, Stuart drew up a list of thirty-two gentlemen "who are to have copies of the Portrait of the President of the United States," to the amount of thirty-nine commissions. Such was the admiration for the President and the confidence in Stuart that those outside of the Philadelphia area, including Benjamin West and the Marquis of Lansdowne in England, placed their orders sight unseen. A Philadelphian on the list, John Vaughan, ordered two portraits, one of which was sent to his father Samuel in England, where it quickly became known through an engraving that appeared in Johann Caspar Lavater's *Essays on Physiognomy*, published in 1798. In consequence, all of the Stuart portraits showing the right side of Washington's face became known as the "Vaughan type."

How many of the thirty-nine portraits Stuart in fact executed cannot be ascertained. Dependability was not a part of his character, however, and his clients were more often surprised than not when he finally delivered a finished portrait. "Genius is always ecentrick, I think," wrote Abigail Adams, who was to wait sixteen years for the delivery of her image. "There is no knowing how to take hold of this Man, nor by what means to prevail upon him to fulfill his engagements."

Among the portraits Gilbert Stuart had not completed in England was a family piece depicting Philadelphia merchant William Bingham, his wife, and his two small daughters in a country setting. It was an important commission, but Stuart, known to throw his brush down at the slightest criticism, may have been offended by the sometimes arrogant William Bingham, or perhaps the children were beyond endurance. But if Bingham had cause to be vexed with Stuart, there was no getting around the fact that the difficult man was far and away the best portrait painter at work in America.

★ *The Patrons*

French exile Charles Maurice de Talleyrand-Périgord, bishop of Autumn, in Maine during the summer of 1795, related a conversation with small-town lawyer Phineas Bruce. If Bruce should go to Philadelphia, Talleyrand asked, would he be pleased to see George Washington? "Why, yes, I shall," replied Bruce, but "added with an excited countenance, 'I should very much like to see Mr. Bingham, who, they say, is so wealthy.'"

William Bingham had laid the basis for his fortune during the American Revolution, when, as agent for the Continental Congress at the French island of Martinique, he combined patriotic service with private trading opportunities. Bingham had been successful in keeping afloat his many enterprises–shipping, banking, land speculation–during a period when many of his associates had become overextended and ended up bankrupt. A conspicuous Federalist, Bingham had advanced from the Pennsylvania legislature to the United States Senate in 1795.

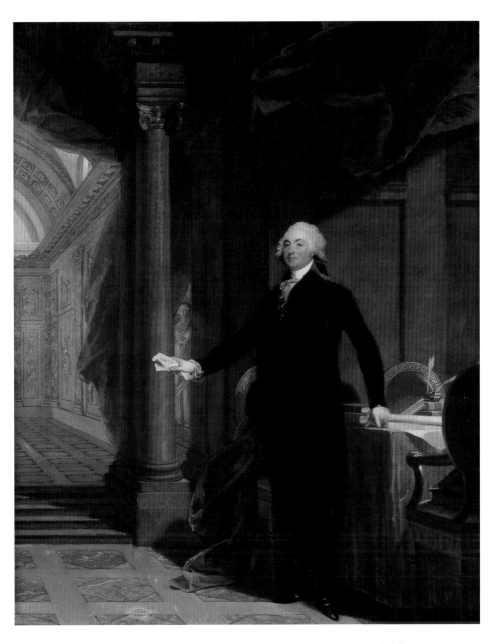

Philadelphia merchant and United States senator William Bingham commissioned Gilbert Stuart to paint a full-length portrait of Washington for presentation to the first Marquis of Lansdowne.

William Bingham
by Gilbert Stuart
Oil on canvas, 1797
ING Barings, London

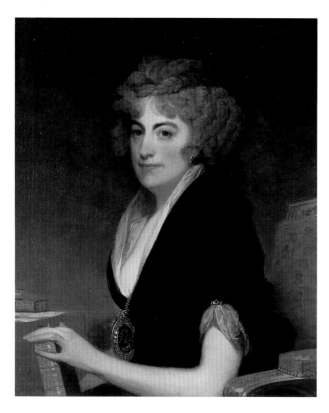

The beautiful Anne (Nancy) Bingham persuaded Washington to have his portrait painted by Gilbert Stuart.

———

Anne Willing Bingham
by Gilbert Stuart
Oil on canvas, 1797
Private collection

Bingham had married sixteen-year-old Anne (Nancy) Willing, who as Quaker Anne Rawle put it, "might set for the Queen of Beauty" in 1780. From 1783 to 1786 the Binghams lived and traveled in Europe, and in England Nancy had been admired even at the Court of St. James's. "I own I felt not a little proud of her," wrote Abigail Adams who, as the wife of the first American minister, had presented her countrywoman to the king and queen. "Is she an American, is she an American?" Mrs. Adams "heard frequently repeated, and even the *ladies* were *obliged to confess* that she was truly an elegant woman."

The Binghams' "pompous mansion house," as John Adams called it, occupied a complete city block in Philadelphia and was modeled after an enlarged version of the Duke of Manchester's London town house. It was, wrote Charles Bulfinch, "in a stile which would be esteemed splendid even in the most luxurious part of Europe. Elegance of construction, white marble staircase, valuable paintings, the richest furniture and the utmost magnificence of decoration makes it a palace." A full-length portrait of Sarah Siddons in her role as the Grecian Daughter hung in the card room; marbles busts of Voltaire and Rousseau, as well as three busts of Benjamin Franklin, were among the adornments in the entrance hall. George Washington, in Philadelphia during the Constitutional Convention, noted in his diary, "Dined and drank Tea at Mr. Binghams in great splender."

Nancy Bingham, polished by her experience with the fashionable world of Europe and adept at emulating the ladies of France in the art of making people feel pleased with themselves, was well equipped to become the uncrowned queen of the Republican Court (as this novel American administration without a king was dubbed) when the federal government moved from New York to Philadelphia in December 1790. She appeared at Martha Washington's first drawing room, held on Christmas Eve. "The dazzling Mrs. Bingham," Abigail Adams wrote, "has certainly given law to the ladies here, in fashion and elegance; their manners and appearance are superior to what I have seen."

It was in vain, Mrs. Bingham told Thomas Jefferson, for American women to contend for the status achieved by the women of France, who "interfere in the politics of the Country, and often give a decided Turn to the Fate of Empires." In her own way, however, she tried to approximate the French Salon in the Philadelphia of the Washington administration, attracting to her drawing room "all that was distinguished and accomplished in the country." The "brilliant balls, sumptuous dinners and constant receptions" aside, John Adams was pleased that he could carry on "something of a political conversation" with Nancy Bingham, whom he pronounced had "more ideas on the subject . . . and a correcter judgement" than he had suspected.

The rivalry for Washington's favor among the ladies of Philadelphia—and it was noted that Washington seemed more at ease when ladies were present—which began when he first came to town as commander of the Continental army, heightened during the years of his presidency. Nancy Bingham's considerable success at the game is affirmed by Robert Gilmor Jr. of Baltimore, who recalled in his memoirs that he had often seen the President "walk arm and arm with Mrs. Bingham round a ball room."

That President Washington, in the midst of political crisis, marched stoically to the painter's chair can be attributed to Mrs. Bingham's adeptness in the "gentle Arts of Persuasion," but surely a further consideration was the destination of the portrait.

★ *The Recipient*

In Paris, Thomas Jefferson had been intrigued by the delight that Nancy Bingham took in European society, and gossiped to James Madison that her husband "had a rage for being presented to great men and had no modesty in the methods by which he could effect it. If he obtained access afterwards, it was with such who were susceptible of impression from the beauty of his wife."

Among those the Binghams had been most anxious to cultivate in Europe was William Petty, the first Marquis of Lansdowne, "having as usual spared no pains to get introduced," as Abigail Adams sniffed. The Adamses' daughter Nabby reported on February 13, 1786, that the Binghams "had dined with Lord Lansdowne, and called to let us know it, I suppose." There is no question that the Binghams were exceedingly flattered by the "civilities" and "polite attention" given them by Lansdowne.

As Lord Shelburne, Lansdowne had worked with William Pitt the Younger to conciliate the colonies with, among other things, the repeal of the Stamp Act and the removal of British troops from Boston. Upon becoming prime minister in July 1782, Shelburne had accepted—albeit with great reluctance—the inevitability

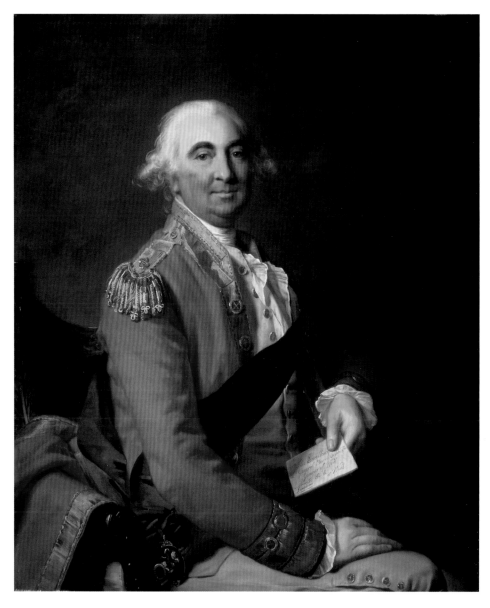

William Petty, first Marquis of Lansdowne, was an enthusiastic supporter of the American cause in the years before and after the Revolution.

William Petty,
first Marquis of Lansdowne
by Jean Laurent Mosnier
Oil on canvas, 1791
By kind permission of the Trustees
of the Bowood Collection

of American independence and sent Benjamin Vaughan (the brother of John and son of Samuel) as his personal adviser at the peace talks in Paris. Shelburne's government concluded the preliminary agreement on November 13, 1782, but the prime minister was forced to resign in February 1783, after the House of Commons passed a vote of censure against the articles of peace. Nonetheless, the important demands of the American negotiators, which were agreed to by Shelburne–gaining independence, a western boundary at the Mississippi River, and fishing rights off Newfoundland–held when the final agreement was signed on September 3, 1783. "This Country has a grateful recollection of the agency your Lordship had in settling the dispute between Great Britain and it," President Washington wrote to Lansdowne in 1791, "and fixing the boundary between them."

Lansdowne, who was regarded in English political circles as a "perfidious and infamous liar," never held office again and conceded in 1786 that he was "growing very insignificant, very fast in the political world." He was so unpopular, Benjamin Vaughan opined, because "his principles were too grand" for other politicians "to comprehend, and therefore it was natural for them not to give him credit for sincerity in maintaining them." Lansdowne's programs went "to the abolition of wars, the promotion of agriculture, the unlimited freedom of trade, and just freedom of man."

William Bingham and Lord Lansdowne had in common a fervent belief in free trade, and Bingham's fourteen-page pamphlet, published in London in 1784, rebutting Lord Sheffield's argument that Americans should be treated as foreigners and excluded from the trade advantages they had enjoyed within the British empire, would have been cause enough for an invitation to dine with Lansdowne.

Lord Lansdowne, a noted patron of literature and the arts, lived in a London town house designed by Robert Adam and filled with antique sculpture and contemporary portraiture. In the dining room (now in the Metropolitan Museum of Art, with the "Room for Company before Dinner" in the Philadelphia Museum of Art), the Binghams would have seen the larger-than-life statues of the Roman emperor Marcus Aurelius and Mercury, the Roman god of commerce, as well as other classical figures recently brought from Rome. Lansdowne's paintings included two Titian renderings of the reformed prostitute Magdalene, a Tintoretto portrait of a cardinal, Andrea del Sarto's *The Holy Family*, an image of the English poet Alexander Pope by Thomas Hudson, a portrait of actor David Garrick by Sir Joshua Reynolds, as well as other works by Reynolds and Thomas Gainsborough.

When thoughts of a gift for Lord Lansdowne–with whom Bingham had continued to correspond–occurred, a grand gesture was called for, with no expense spared. To be worthy of a place in the Lansdowne collection, no ordinary portrait would suffice.

★ *The Portrait*

On April 12, 1796, President George Washington, as was his custom, recorded the weather in his diary: "Thick morning, but clear afterwards, rather cool wind Easterly in the morning & westerly afterwards." He makes no mention of his appoinment with Gilbert Stuart. In fact the only reference to Stuart (other than the April 11 note) to be found among Washington's papers is his January 7, 1797, diary entry: "Road to German Town with Mrs. Washington to see Mr. Stuarts paintings."

Most people found sitting for Gilbert Stuart, with his waggish wit (not to mention puns) and store of anecdotes, to be a pleasurable experience. "I should like to sit to Stuart from the first of January to the last of December," John Adams said in his old age, "for he lets me do just what I please and keeps me constantly amused by his conversation." It was not so with George Washington. In one of his several accounts of the sitting, the artist related that he had said to the President, "Now, sir, you must let me forget that you are General Washington and that I am Stuart the painter." Washington, according to Stuart, replied, "Mr. Stuart need never feel the need of forgetting who he is or who General Washington is." As soon as the President settled into the painter's chair, Stuart recounted, "an apathy seemed to seize him, and a vacuity seemed to spread over his countenance most appalling to the painter." Stuart, the practiced raconteur, "made several fruitless attempts to awaken the heroic spirit in him by talking of battles, but in vain; he next tried to warm up the patriot and sage by turning the conversation to the republican ages of antiquity; this was equally unsuccessful." Talk of horses and agriculture produced a terse response, and at length Washington responded to a hoary joke, causing Stuart to boast afterwards that he then "had him on a pivot and could manage him nicely."

In later years, Gilbert Stuart "talked freely of Washington," the art critic and novelist John Neal related, "of his large features and stately bearing, and of the signs he saw, in the massive jaw, the wide nostrils, and large eye-sockets, that he was a man of almost ungovernable passions and indomitable will."

Fortunately for Washington, Stuart painted with great rapidity, frequently requiring only two sittings and seldom more than four or five. Philadelphia lawyer Horace Binney remembered that Stuart finished his head except for the eyes in one sitting, and required his presence but one more time.

The President was not asked to pose for the figure, and memories vary on who served as the mannequin. A daughter of Philadelphia alderman Michael Keppele claimed the honor for her father, who was twenty-four years old at the time. Martha Washington's grandson, George Washington Parke Custis, said it was a man named Smith, a smaller man than Washington, who owned the house Stuart rented on Chestnut Street. The Smith in question was W. Moore Smith, and his son, writing in November 1858, said that his father "was certainly a more graceful man in his proportions, and carriage, than Michael Keppele." Another had it that actor-comedian John Pollard Moreton stood for the figure because of his "natural grace."

The candidate for the most grace, it should be said, was the Vicomte de Noailles, erstwhile dancing partner of Marie Antoinette, for whom a Bingham connection put in the claim. Noailles, who had fought with Washington in the American Revolution, was an exile from revolutionary France and occupied a third-story room at the end of the Bingham garden. However, since Noailles was in Maine with the Binghams from June 13 to September 22, 1796, his availability for the Lansdowne portrait was limited, although he may have posed for different full-lengths ordered after Washington's death by the legislatures of Connecticut and Rhode Island.

When George Washington was first inaugurated as President in New York in 1789, he made a point of being dressed in a brown suit of domestic cloth from the Hartford manufactory. That gesture of encouragement to the infant American textile industry had long since been cast aside, and for ceremonial occasions he donned the black velvet costume ordered from New York tailor (and former patriotic spy) Hercules Mulligan. In the words of a Philadelphia woman who watched the President deliver his annual address to Congress, Washington appeared–very much as Stuart shows him–"in his own *dignity and moral grandeur–erect, serene, and majestic*; his costume was a full suit of black velvet; his hair blanched by time and powdered to snowy whiteness; a dress sword at his side and his hat in his hand." The cocked hat was remembered by another contemporary as "trimmed with [a] cockade in it, and the edges adorned with a black feather about an inch deep."

Stuart positioned Washington in a stance suitable for grand-manner European portraiture, a pose that was later interpreted in a newspaper description as a representation of the President "in the dignified attitude, of delivering his last farewell," a fictional scene, since the address was never given, but rather published in the *American Daily Advertiser* on September 19, 1796. Nevertheless, retirement from office was the desire of Washington's heart, and within a few weeks of the April sitting, he would send a draft of what became known as the "Farewell Address" to Alexander Hamilton for reworking. Whether intended or not, the posture and gesture is in keeping with his exhortation for national unity and a warning against the "insidious wiles of foreign influence."

Likewise, the artistic convention of the rainbow, interpreted as a sign that the "great and tremendous storms" that had frequently prevailed in the political life of the country "have abated," was–by the time the portrait was finished–an accurate assessment of the moment. As he stood before the Congress for the last time in December 1796, Washington recalled the uncertainty of "the period when the Administration of the present form of Government commenced," and exulted "I cannot omit the occasion, to congratulate you and my Country, on the success of the experiment."

The composition and background of the portrait originated with Stuart's portfolio of European engravings but was much altered to reflect the symbolism of the

American republic. The furniture legs–doubtless imaginative–are in the shape of a tapering bundle of fasci, the Roman emblem of authority, a design perhaps inspired by the mace of the House of Representatives. This was described in 1793 as "somewhat in the form of the ancient Roman Fasces, it consists of thirteen arrows bound together, and an eagle on the top." In any case, the eagles, grasping in their talons thirteen arrows, are derived from the Great Seal of the United States, as is the shield on the "state chair" (as it was called in the London press), its thirteen red and white vertical stripes held together by the broad blue band, symbolizing the union of the individual states.

Genuine enough is the Oushak Anatolian carpet. The story is told that Henry Daniel McCormick, a friend of Stuart's, came upon the artist carrying a turkey rug for his painting room and exclaimed, "You extravagant dog, why did you not buy a kidderminister [an ingrain carpet used as a substitute for the expensive Orientals] which is cheap, and would have answered as well?" Stuart replied, "McCormick, you will see some day if I have done right."

The silver inkstand in the neoclassical boat shape and faintly displaying the Washington family coat of arms may or may not be a real object. The crouching hounds bring to mind Plutarch's (a much-read author among eighteenth-century Americans) observation that dogs symbolize "the conservative watchful, philosophical principle of life," a sentiment certainly espoused by the Federalists.

Books under the table are lettered *General Orders* and *American Revolution*, references to Washington's eight-and-a-half years as commander in chief of the Continental army. A third book, *Constitution & Laws of the United States*, can be taken as a reminder of Washington's centrality at the Constitutional Convention, where it was recognized that the powers of the executive would not have been so great "had not many of the members cast their eyes toward General Washington as President; and shaped their Ideas of the Powers to be given to a President, by their opinions of his Virtue." On the table are *Journal of Congress* and *Federalist*. This last was the bound volume of the newspaper essays penned by James Madison, Alexander Hamilton, and John Jay to explain and promote the ratification of the Constitution. The book was worthy "as claiming a most distinguished place in my library," Washington told Hamilton, adding that this "work will merit the notice of Posterity; because in it are candidly discussed the principles of freedom & the topics of government, which will be always interesting to mankind so long as they shall be connected in Civil Society."

Stuart, the great procrastinator, was uncharacteristically diligent about getting beyond the head and completing the whole painting. "I have sent by the present opportunity a full length Portrait of the President," William Bingham alerted United States minister to England Rufus King on November 29, 1796.

It is executed by Stewart (who is well known in London) with a great deal of enthusiasm, and in his best manner, & does great credit to the American Artist. It is intended as a Present on the part of Mrs. Bingham to Lord Landsdown. As a warm Friend of the United States and a great admirer of the President, it can not have a better Destination.

Lord Lansdowne did not write instantly to thank Mrs. Bingham because of "an almost unceasing pain in my head," he explained to Major William Jackson, Bingham's business associate. "But I have received the picture, which is in every respect worthy of the original. I consider it as a very magnificent compliment, and the respect I have for both Mr. and Mrs. Bingham will always enhance the value of it to me and my family." In reference to the successful ratification of the Treaty of Amity, Commerce, and Navigation, Lansdowne added, "I cannot express to you the satisfaction I have felt in seeing the forts given up"–that is, the British northwestern posts on American soil, which were finally relinquished by the midsummer of 1796. "The deed is done, and a strong foundation laid for eternal amity between England and America."

Lord Lansdowne, with Washington's voluntary relinquishment of office fresh in mind, intoned, "General Washington's conduct is above all praise. He has left a noble example to sovereigns and nations, present and to come." He continued, "If I was not too old, I would go to Virginia to do him homage." Washington had been equally polite when, in writing to Lansdowne in 1794, he had remarked that it would give him the "truest satisfaction" to have the "opportunity of welcoming you to a Country, to the esteem of which you have so just a title."

An account of Lansdowne's gift appeared in London's *Oracle and Public Advertiser* of May 15, 1797. Calling the portrait "one of the finest pictures we have seen since the death of Reynolds," the London critic went on:

To many a description of the person of General Washington will be new: the picture enables us from its fidelity to describe it very correctly. The figure is above the middle height [Washington was more than six feet tall], well proportioned, and exceedingly grace-ful. The countenance is mild and yet forcible. The eye, of a light grey, is rendered marking by a brow to which physiognomy attaches the sign of power. The forehead is ample, the nose aquiline, the mouth regular and persuasive.

That the portrait was a perfect resemblance was attested to by Lansdowne's eldest son, Lord Wycombe, who had met President Washington at Philadelphia in 1791.

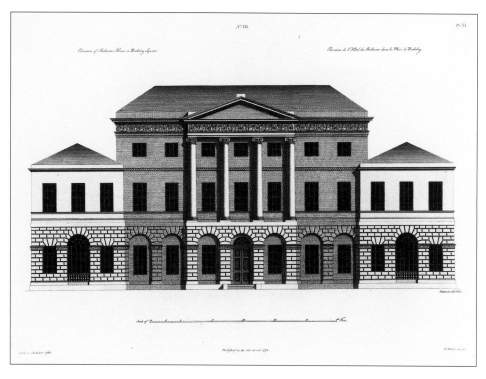

Lord Lansdowne, a noted patron of literature and the arts, hung the Washington portrait in his London town house designed by Robert Adam.

Elevation of Shelburne House, 1778. Library of Congress, Washington, D.C.

Stuart, to be sure, took care to gloss over the scars left by the smallpox Washington had contracted when he accompanied his half-brother Lawrence to Barbados in the early 1750s. As to Washington's light grayish-blue eyes, the artist had painted them of a deeper hue, saying "in a hundred years they will have faded to the right color."

Lord Lansdowne hung the portrait in the elegant library ("circular and with domes at both ends") of his London house on Berkeley Square, which was embellished with a stunning array of painting and sculpture. "The pictures," a visitor related in 1804 "are a full length of Washington, a fine head of Rubens; a small but beautiful Claude, a seaport, sun setting, and a dark woody island, combining both his favourite subjects, two charming heads by Murillo; a noble landscape, but small, by Poussin." The prizes of the Lansdowne art collection were the ancient marbles from Greece and Rome, and among the "exquisite statues" was "Cincinnatus tying on his sandal," a particularly appropriate accompaniment to the image of Washington. The President was often compared to the Roman Cincinnatus, who left his plow to save the Roman republic and then promptly relinquished the power of office to return to private life.

★ *The Aftermath*

During the summer of 1796 Gilbert Stuart moved to Germantown, seven miles outside of Philadelphia, and set up his painting room in a stable on the rented property there. It had been necessary, the artist explained, to retire "from the busy interruptions" of the city in order to undertake the many orders for copies of his monumental Washington portrait. Young Robert Gilmor of Baltimore, who came by in July 1797 with a letter of introduction from the Vicomte de Noailles, was graciously received, and he detailed the visit in his journal:

> The Picture he had there of the President was the first copy he had made of the celebrated full length which he had painted for Mr. Bingham intended as a present to the Marquis of Lansdown. It was supposed one of the finest portraits that ever was painted. This copy was for Mr. Binghams own use and from which Stewart told us he had engaged to finish copies to [the] amount of 70 or 80,000 Drs. at the rate 600 Drs. a copy.

An amazed Gilmor (soon to become one of America's pioneer art collectors) reflected, "This circumstance is unique in the history of painting, that the portrait of one man should be sought after in such a degree as to be copied by the original artist such a number of times and for such an amount."

However many orders for copies of the Lansdowne Stuart actually received, it is inconceivable that the number was more than one hundred. Equally incredulous is the notion that Stuart–who was easily bored by details beyond the face–could bring himself to replicate the elaborate full-length in any great numbers.

One person who did receive a copy was New York merchant William Constable, a former Philadelphian notorious in Republican circles for having profited greatly through speculation in government securities. In the course of having his own portrait painted, Constable saw the painting in progress and insisted he must have one for his new house on Broadway. Constable paid Stuart $500 for the portrait on July 4, 1797.

The Bingham replica of the Lansdowne, it turned out, was not for the embellishment of the Philadelphia mansion house, but rather for the white marble country house on the west bank of the Schuylkill River, called "Lansdowne" by colonial lieutenant governor John Penn long before William Bingham purchased it in April 1797. In September of that year Robert Gilmor Jr. came upon Gilbert Stuart painting the whole family in the library.

Nancy Bingham died of consumption in 1801, "her brilliant career . . . ended" at the age of thirty-seven, and William Bingham died at Bath, England, in 1804, with Lord Lansdowne answering a summons to his deathbed. In the inventory of Bingham's estate, filed by the executors in 1807, the Washington full-length portrait is specifically mentioned as being at Lansdowne.

Of the many renditions of the "Lansdowne-type," only three of the canvases (all of them ordered for private homes) are, without dispute, completely by the hand of Gilbert Stuart–the original delivered to the Marquis of Lansdowne; the Bingham replica given to the Pennsylvania Academy of the Fine Arts by the Bingham estate in 1811 (see page 97); and the replica paid for by William Constable, now in the Brooklyn Museum of Art.

We do know that General Charles Cotesworth Pinckney, in Philadelphia in September 1796 on his way to his post as minister to France, ordered a Lansdowne portrait for presentation to the French Republic and requested that Secretary of State Timothy Pickering settle with Stuart when the full-length was finished. Pickering accordingly paid Stuart $500 on July 22, 1797, but since the French Directory, affronted by the Jay Treaty, had refused to receive Pinckney, the picture was not sent abroad. Pinckney repeatedly asked Stuart to account for the portrait, which he presumed to have been painted, but the artist never answered his letters. There is speculation that Stuart–who played the part of scoundrel in more than one instance–sold the portrait a second time and it may have been the full-length "Portrait of General Washington (large as life)" that Gardner Baker, proprietor of the American Museum in New York, displayed in February 1798. "Mr. Stewart is justly celebrated as the greatest painter of the age, and Washington is his hobby-horse," Baker advertised.

> Those who have not had the pleasure of seeing our illustrious Washington, now have the opportunity of gratifying themselves, and those who have seen him, will here again realize all his noble dignity and triumphs, bestowing his good advice to his country-men. He is surrounded with allegorical emblems of his public life in the service of his country.

To add to the confusion surrounding the Lansdowne-type portraits, a number of artists made copies of the Stuart work, the most flagrant of whom was the English landscape artist William Winstanley. Winstanley, as Stuart tells the tale, visited him in Germantown and announced that he had painted six copies of the full-length Washington. "It would enhance their value, you know, if I could say that you had given them the last touch," Stuart quoted Winstanley as saying. "Now, sir, all you have to do is to ride to town, and give each of them a tap, you know, with your riding-switch." Stuart replied, he let it be known, by saying, "You will please walk down stairs, sir, very quickly, or I shall throw you out at the window."

In 1800 the committee in charge of furnishing the new executive mansion agreed to the purchase (at a cost of $800, including the frame) of a "portrait full length of the late Genl. Washington by Stewart." However, Gilbert Stuart, on a visit to Washington in August 1802, it was reported, "denies most pointedly having painted the picture in the President's House." The argument as to whether Stuart or Winstanley (or even someone else) painted the canvas in the White House has continued to this day, but the fact remains that Gilbert Stuart's Lansdowne image of the first President of the United States is a fixture in the nation's patrimony. Dolley Madison realized its iconic importance when, in the perilous moments before the British army entered Washington in August 1814, she refused to flee until the "precious portrait" of George Washington was broken out of its frame and carried off to safekeeping.

For Stuart, the aftermath of the important Lansdowne commission left a bitter taste. "Stewart has been much disappointed in his Hopes relative to Profits, which he expected to receive from this Picture," William Bingham informed Rufus King on July 10, 1797.

> He had wrote to his friend West, requesting him to engage an able artist to execute an Engraving therefrom, which, from the general admiration the picture attracted, might have been disposed of to great advantage in this Country. He has not heard from Mr. West, & he is fearful that Lord Landsdown's obliging character may induce him to permit some other artist to take off the Impression.

A print of the Lansdowne executed by James Heath was published in London just weeks after Washington's death in December 1799. According to Stuart's version of the story, the first he knew of it was when he came upon the engravings for sale in Dobson's bookstore in Philadelphia during the summer of 1800.

Among the few papers left by Stuart is an undated draft of a letter addressed to Lord Lansdowne, in which Stuart declared that he had looked to an engraving of the picture by an artist of talent as a means of rescuing him from debt and providing for his numerous family. "It was therefore, with peculiar pleasure," Stuart wrote, "that I found myself invited by Mr. Bingham to take the portrait of President Washington, to be presented to your Lordship." He had complied immediately with Bingham's request, but "expressly stipulated with his agent in the transaction, that no copy should be taken of the picture, nor should any engraving be allowed but with my consent, and for my benefit."

In 1825 Stuart related to the young artist James B. Longacre that he had called upon William Bingham, reminded him of his copyright stipulation, and asked "how he proposed to compensate him for the injury he had sustained by the publication of the print." Bingham cooly asked, "Have you anything to show for it?" whereupon Stuart left him "abruptly and indignantly without further remark."

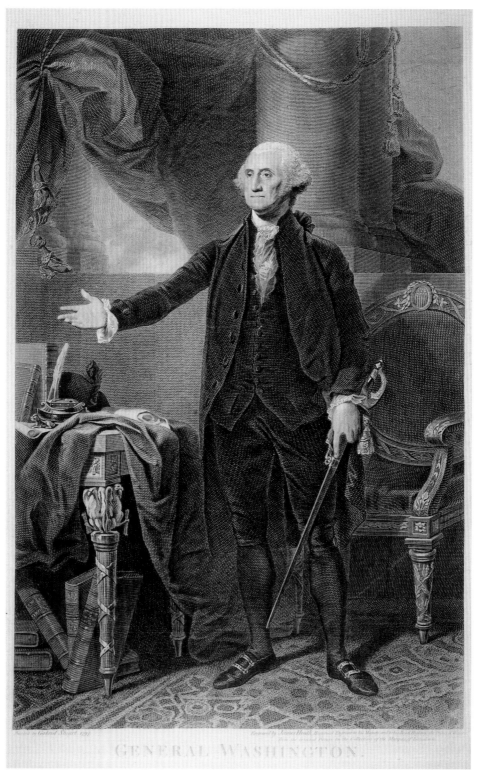

GENERAL WASHINGTON.

*James Heath's print of the Lansdowne painting was published in London just weeks after
Washington's death in December 1799.*

George Washington
by James Heath
Engraving, 1800
National Portrait Gallery,
Smithsonian Institution

★ *The Change of Hands*

After the Marquis of Lansdowne's death in 1805, part of the collection in his London house was auctioned at a two-day sale in March 1806. The English sculptor Joseph Nollekens called out excitedly to a friend that the auctioneer "has just knocked down General Washington, Stuart's picture. Well, what do you think? it fetched a great deal more than any modern picture ever brought by auction before, for he has just sold it at Lord Lansdown's for 540£ 15s!"

The successful bidder was the Massachusetts-born merchant-banker Samuel Williams. President Washington had named Williams as the American consul at Hamburg, Germany, in 1796, telling Secretary of State Timothy Pickering (Williams's uncle), "it is fortunate that so eligible a character as Mr. Samuel Williams of Salem" was available for the appointment. Later Williams was moved to London, where he served until dismissed by the Jefferson administration in 1801.

Williams lived and did "an immense business" at 13 Finsbury Square, in the East End of London, where he had a small art collection. He was known for his kindness and hospitality to visiting Americans, particularly young artists. Washington Allston, who painted his portrait, called him "my excellent friend."

Gilbert Stuart had settled in Boston in 1805 and was acquainted with Samuel Williams's brother Timothy. On March 9, 1823, Stuart gave Timothy Williams George Washington's note of April 11, 1796. "In looking over my papers to find one that had the Signature of George Washington," Timothy Williams wrote to Stuart's dictation:

> I found this asking me when he should sit for his portrait, which is now owned, by Samuel Williams of London, I have thought it proper, it should be his especially as he owns the only original painting I ever made of Washington except one I own myself. I painted a third but rubbed it out. I now present [this] to his Brother Timo. Williams, for sd Samuel.

Timothy added "N. B. Mr. Stuart painted in ye *winter season* his first portrait of Washington, but destroyed it. The next portrait was ye one now owned by S. Williams; the third, Mr. S now has–two only remain as above stated." In the presence of three witnesses Stuart added his signature in a tremulous hand, bringing to mind John Neagle's 1825 observation that Stuart's "hands shook at times so violently, that I wondered how he could place his brush where his mind directed."

The image Stuart claimed he "rubbed out" is presumably the original of the Vaughan series, to which Stuart never returned once he had painted Washington facing left. The portrait that Stuart himself owned–the basis for his many bust portraits of Washington–was the unfinished "Athenaeum," called such because on its purchase from Stuart's widow it was presented to the Boston Athenaeum.

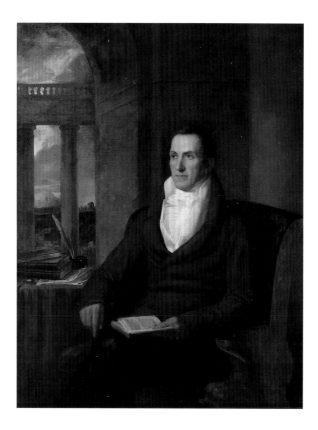

Washington, according to George Washington Parke Custis, posed for this last at the behest of Martha Washington, but the artist resisted all entreaties that it be delivered to her.

Samuel Williams's "great American banking house" failed in 1825, and his creditors decided to dispose of the portrait (together with the Washington note) in a lottery. The winner, in 1827, was John Delaware Lewis, an English merchant doing business at St. Petersburg. As engraver John Sartain remembered events, the raffle ticket had been bought for Lewis by a subordinate member of the firm during his absence from London, "and when he learned of the purchase he had been greatly incensed, and threatened to repudiate the transaction. He was calmed by a warning whispered in his ear that he was risking by this course the loss of a lucrative trade with America."

The American artist Charles C. Leslie, who was familiar with the portrait when it was in Williams's possession, thought it the finest full-length of Washington in existence. "How fortunate it was that a painter existed in the time of Washington, who could hand him down to us looking like a gentleman," Leslie exclaimed. In 1836 Leslie related that Louis McLane, Andrew Jackson's minister to England, had proposed to his former colleagues in Congress that the picture be purchased for the nation, "but the measure was thrown out." The portrait was still in London, and Leslie thought it could be purchased for seven or eight hundred guineas.

However, the Lansdowne remained in the Lewis family, descending in 1841 to the junior John Delaware Lewis, who served in Parliament as a member of the Liberal Party and who was the author of books written in French as well as English.

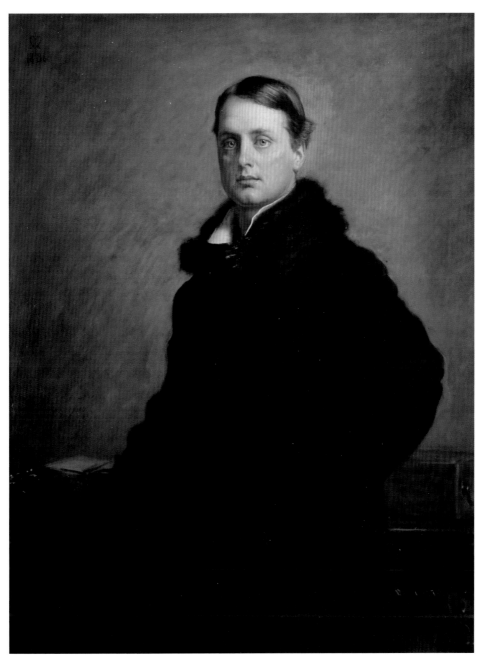

In 1889 Archibald Philip Primrose, the fifth Earl of Rosebery, purchased the Lansdowne painting. It remained in his family until its sale to the National Portrait Gallery in 2001.

The fifth Earl of Rosebery
by Sir John Everett Millais
Oil on canvas, 1884
The Earl of Rosebery

Prompted by an American uncle, Lewis lent the portrait to the Philadelphia Centennial Exposition in 1876 at an insurance value that "was something enormous." The Washington note was sent along with the portrait, and John Sartain, chief of the exposition's Bureau of Art, mentioned in his autobiography, "This interesting document I had fixed securely behind a thick plate glass and fastened below the canvas."

After Lewis's death in 1884, the portrait came into the hands of Herman LeRoy Lewis. In May 1889, the Lansdowne was purchased by Archibald Philip Primrose, the fifth Earl of Rosebery–for two thousand guineas, according to Sartain. From his schoolboy days, Rosebery had been an enthusiastic collector of "books, pictures, old silver and young horses." He married Hannah, the only child of Baron Meyer de Rothschild in 1878, and through her inherited Mentmore Towers and the spectacular Rothschild array of pictures and decorative arts.

In 1873, when he was twenty-six, Rosebery had toured the United States and was much taken with George Washington's correspondence and account book "all kept in his own neat handwriting," then on view at the State Department. "One I noticed," Rosebery recorded in his journal, "was ordering his London tailor to send him clothes and telling the tailor in case the measure is lost that he is six feet high and proportioned for that height." Rosebery went on to comment that portraits of Washington by Stuart "are considered to have been very flattering."

Active in the Liberal Party, Rosebery served as prime minister from 1892 to 1895. Besides political involvement, he was the author of biographies of Napoleon, William Pitt, Lord Chatham, and Lord Randolph Churchill. In his book on Pitt, published in 1892, Rosebery observed that Lord Shelburne, "who, if not the friend, had at least the courage to be the admirer, of the successful rebel Washington, with whom he had to sign peace."

In London, Rosebery lived at 38 Berkeley Square, where he created a gallery of famous statesmen of the eighteenth century in his dining room, hanging alongside the Washington Lansdowne portraits of William Pitt by Sir Thomas Lawrence, Lord Rockingham by Sir Joshua Reynolds, as well as images of Lord Chatham, Lord North, and Admiral Rodney. Rosebery, a collector of Napoleoniana, also had on view Jacques-Louis David's full-length portrait of Napoleon, the man who famously said after his fall from power, "They wanted me to be another Washington."

★ *The National Portrait Gallery*

In preparation for the 1968 public opening of the National Portrait Gallery, Charles Nagel, the Gallery's first director, sought out "a picture of the father of our country from which the collection would flow forward and back in the point of time." Such was Gilbert Stuart's noble Lansdowne representation, the original of which was by then owned by the sixth Earl of Rosebery.

Smithsonian Secretary Dillon Ripley was in enthusiastic agreement that the Gallery should investigate the possibility of acquiring the portrait, and in a letter

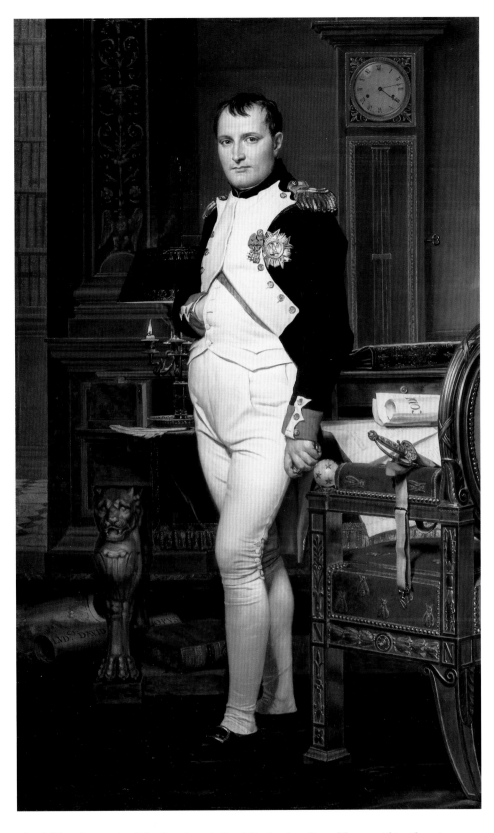

This full-length portrait of Napoleon hung in Lord Rosebery's gallery of famous eighteenth-century statesmen, as did the Lansdowne painting of Washington.

The Emperor Napoleon in His Study at the Tuileries by Jacques-Louis David, oil on canvas, 1812.
National Gallery of Art, Washington, D.C.; Samuel H. Kress Collection

requesting a loan of three months for the opening exhibition, he added, "if there would be any chance of the portrait's remaining here permanently as part of our collection, I can imagine nothing that would launch the Gallery with greater luster, or be a happier event in the artistic history of our respective countries."

"I am afraid I cannot send the portrait of Washington," Lord Rosebery said in a terse reply on March 20, 1967, adding, "there is no question of the portrait being disposed of." Despite opinions that the eighty-six-year-old Lord Rosebery's "No" really meant "No," Ripley sought the help of Admiral Lord Mountbatten, with whom he had served in the South Pacific during World War II. In reply to Mountbatten's plea for reconsideration, Rosebery informed Ripley that the picture now belonged to his son, Lord Primrose of Dalmeny House in West Lothian, Scotland, to whom he had passed over all his Scottish possessions. He would relay the request, but "I rather doubt his lending the picture. Some years ago I lent it to an American Exhibition (I forgot the exact one) [the George Washington Bicentennial Historical Loan Exhibition at the Corcoran Gallery of Art in 1932]. Again, only two years ago it was taken from an inaccessible position in the Musicians Gallery at Barnbougle [a reconstructed seventeenth-century castle on the grounds of Dalmeny House] to be copied for another of the American Universities."

But Mountbatten's letter did the trick, and Lord Primrose, although reluctant to lend the portrait, decided that "this does seem a suitable occasion." An exultant Charles Nagel hastened to tell Primrose, "To have a distinguished portrait of the father of our country with the wonderful history of this one is the sort of thing one dreams of for an opening exhibition such as ours." The portrait, placed to greet visitors as they ascended the grand stairway to the second floor, became literally the center of attention in the new Portrait Gallery.

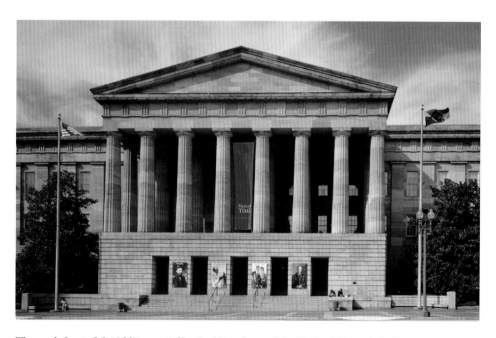

The south front of the Old Patent Office Building, home of the National Portrait Gallery.

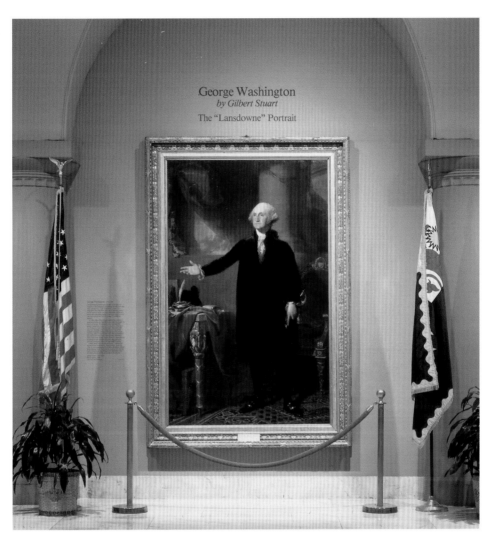

The Lansdowne portrait of Washington hung in its place of honor in the National Portrait Gallery's second-floor rotunda, before the Old Patent Office Building closed for renovation in January 2000.

"It is my considered opinion that the Lansdowne Washington is *the* American portrait, and would constitute an incomparable cornerstone for the collection of the National Portrait Gallery," Marvin Sadik declared as he prepared to take over as the Gallery's second director. "I have no hesitation in saying that the picture is the one American portrait above all others this nation would most like to own." Every inch of the large-scale canvas is distinguished, Sadik enthused, by "the subtlety in physiognomic characterization and the sparkling brushwork throughout."

Sadik's hope, and the hope of the third director, Alan Fern, that the Gallery would be able to acquire the portrait did not materialize, but the offer of a long-term long was gratefully implemented, and the Lansdowne painting remained in its honored place until the Gallery closed for a massive renovation in January 2000.

In 1992 the seventh Earl of Rosebery passed the ownership of the painting to his eldest son, Lord Dalmeny, who in October 2000 told the Gallery that he was putting the picture on the market at a price of $20 million. Dalmeny, who was not yet born when the portrait was loaned to the Gallery, wanted it known that he was "extremely happy with the way the National Portrait Gallery had cared for the painting and believes it is [in] a wonderful location." Dalmeny gave the Gallery the exclusive right of purchase, but only until April 1, 2001.

After an intensive search of more than four months failed to bring forth a donor, the Portrait Gallery decided to let the public know–on Washington's birthday–that a national treasure was in danger of being lost. "We think that the person who will buy this for the nation will not be automatically known to us," Marc Pachter, the Gallery's fourth director, explained. "This is not the universe of art collectors but the universe of patriots. There are many patriots who are not associated with museums."

And so it was that Fred W. Smith read about the Lansdowne in the *Wall Street Journal* on February 23, and the next Tuesday he saw Marc Pachter make a plea for a donor on the *Today Show*. Smith is chairman of the Donald W. Reynolds Foundation, established by the founder and principal owner of the Donrey Media Group, a vast communications and media empire. Reynolds, who died in 1993 at the age of eighty-six, left most of his billions of dollars to the foundation, whose activities are centered in Nevada, Arkansas, and Oklahoma, awarding grants in the areas of journalism training, cardiovascular clinical research, and studies on aging.

Smith, struck by what he recognized as a "patriotic emergency," had foundation president Steve Anderson contact the Smithsonian, and on March 3 Pachter met with Smith and foundation staff at the foundation's headquarters in Las Vegas. That very day the trustees were polled by telephone and agreed that this was a chance "to give back to the American people." An agreement was reached, not only to provide funds for the purchase of the Washington Lansdowne, but also for a dedicated space for it in the renovated Patent Office Building and for a grand national tour, bringing the portrait of the father of the country to areas of the United States beyond the imagination of Americans in the age of Washington.

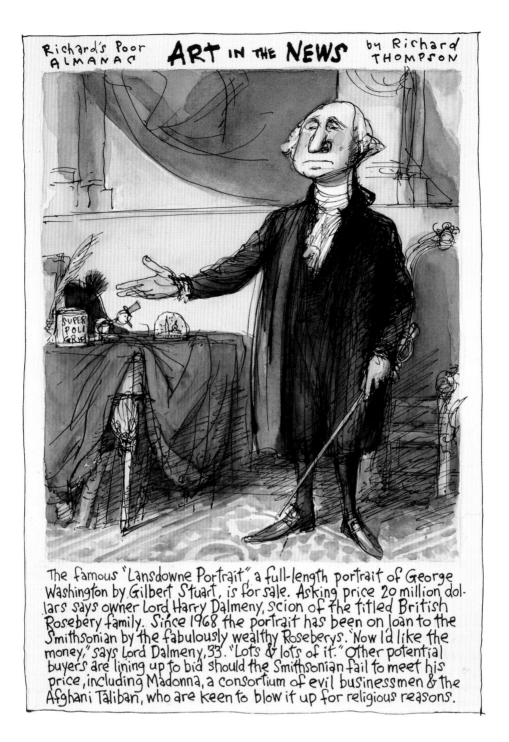

The famous "Lansdowne Portrait", a full-length portrait of George Washington by Gilbert Stuart, is for sale. Asking price 20 million dollars says owner Lord Harry Dalmeny, scion of the titled British Rosebery family. Since 1968 the portrait has been on loan to the Smithsonian by the fabulously wealthy Roseberys. "Now I'd like the money," says Lord Dalmeny, 33. "Lots & lots of it." Other potential buyers are lining up to bid should the Smithsonian fail to meet his price, including Madonna, a consortium of evil businessmen & the Afghani Taliban, who are keen to blow it up for religious reasons.

Richard Thompson's political cartoon lamented the possible fate of the Lansdowne image if a donor was not found to help the Portrait Gallery purchase it.

Richard's Poor Almanac:
Art in the News
by Richard Thompson
Ink and watercolor drawing, 2001
Originally published in
the *Washington Post*
National Portrait Gallery,
Smithsonian Institution

"We felt, as I am sure every American did, that it would be a tragedy to lose this original portrait of our founding father," said Smith in making the announcement of the foundation's gift on March 13, 2001. "Our benefactor, Donald W. Reynolds, believed that every American owed a debt of gratitude to those that came before us. He also felt that we have an obligation to keep the symbols of our country's principles for those in the future."

Comments on Sources

The literature surrounding George Washington is, to state the obvious, rich and voluminous. Of primary importance are the published manuscript sources: *The Writings of George Washington, from the Original Manuscript Sources, 1745–1799*, edited by John C. Fitzpatrick (39 vols.; Washington, D.C.: Government Printing Office, 1931–1944); the new edition of *The Papers of George Washington*, edited by W. W. Abbott, Dorothy Twohig et. al. (Charlottesville: University Press of Virginia, 1983–); and the extant *Diaries of George Washington*, the six volumes edited by Donald Jackson and Dorothy Twohig (Charlottesville: University Press of Virginia, 1976–1979). The most comprehensive Washington biography is Douglas Southall Freeman's six-volume *George Washington* (New York: Scribner's, 1949–1957), with a seventh volume completed by John Alexander Carroll and Mary Wells Ashworth as *George Washington: First in Peace* (New York: Scribner's, 1967). James Thomas Flexner's four-volume *George Washington* (Boston: Little, Brown, 1974) is likewise a sweeping treatment of Washington's life. Two recent interpretations are Richard Norton Smith's *Patriarch: George Washington and the New American Nation* (Boston: Houghton Mifflin, 1993) and Richard Brookhiser's *Founding Father: Rediscovering George Washington* (New York: Free Press, 1996.)

Washington's contemporaries had a great many things to say about him, and some of the more trenchant observations are to be found in *The Spur of Fame: Dialogues of John Adams and Benjamin Rush, 1805–1813*, edited by John A. Schutz and Douglass Adair (San Marino, Calif.: Huntington Library, 1966). Henry T. Tuckerman's *The Character and Portraits of Washington* (New York: Putnam, 1859) is one of several sources for quotations on Washington's appearance, including observations by Washington's adopted grandson, George Washington Parke Custis.

When it comes to Gilbert Stuart, the primary source material is all but nonexistent. Much of the Stuart lore comes from William Dunlap, who knew Stuart in London and later in Boston, and who assiduously gathered anecdotes from the many artists who had come into contact with the garrulous Stuart. Dunlap's gossipy treatment of Stuart in *A History of the Rise and Progress of the Arts of Design* (first published in 1834 and since reissued), so irritated Stuart's youngest daughter, Jane, that she requested George C. Mason to undertake *The Life and Works of Gilbert Stuart*, published in 1879 (reprinted in 1972). Jane herself wrote a series of articles for *Scribner's Monthly* in 1876 and 1877–"The Stuart Portraits of Washington" (vol. 12), "The Youth of Gilbert Stuart" (vol. 13), and "Anecdotes of Gilbert Stuart" (vol. 14). Jane, however, was not born until 1812 and so was not a witness to most of what she related. William T. Whitley's *Gilbert Stuart* (Cambridge: Harvard University Press, 1932) contains invaluable information from contemporary periodicals and records, as well as the sole mention of the Washington portrait in place in Lord Lansdowne's library. Printed in John Hill Morgan and Mantle Fielding's *The Life Portraits of Washington and Their Replicas* (Philadelphia: printed for the subscribers, 1931) are Gardner Baker's 1798 advertisements describing the full-length Washington portrait.

The definitive treatment of the Binghams is Robert C. Alberts's *Golden Voyage: The Life and Times of William Bingham* (Boston: Houghton Mifflin, 1969). Lord Shelburne's role in the negotiations bringing the American Revolution to a close is addressed in *John Jay: The Winning of the Peace, Unpublished Papers, 1780–1784*, edited by Richard B. Morris and Ene Sirvet (New York: Harper & Row, 1980).

William Bingham's letters of November 29, 1796, and July 10, 1797, to Rufus King are to be found in volume two of *The Life and Correspondence of Rufus King*, edited by Charles R. King (New York: G. P. Putnam's Sons, 1896). Lord Lansdowne's letter of March 5, 1797, to William Jackson is printed in Charles Henry Hart's article, "Stuart's Lansdowne Portrait of Washington" in *Harper's New Monthly Magazine* 93 (August 1896). Robert Gilmor's account of his visit to Gilbert Stuart's painting room appears in the April 1892 *Bulletin of the Public Library of the City of Boston*.

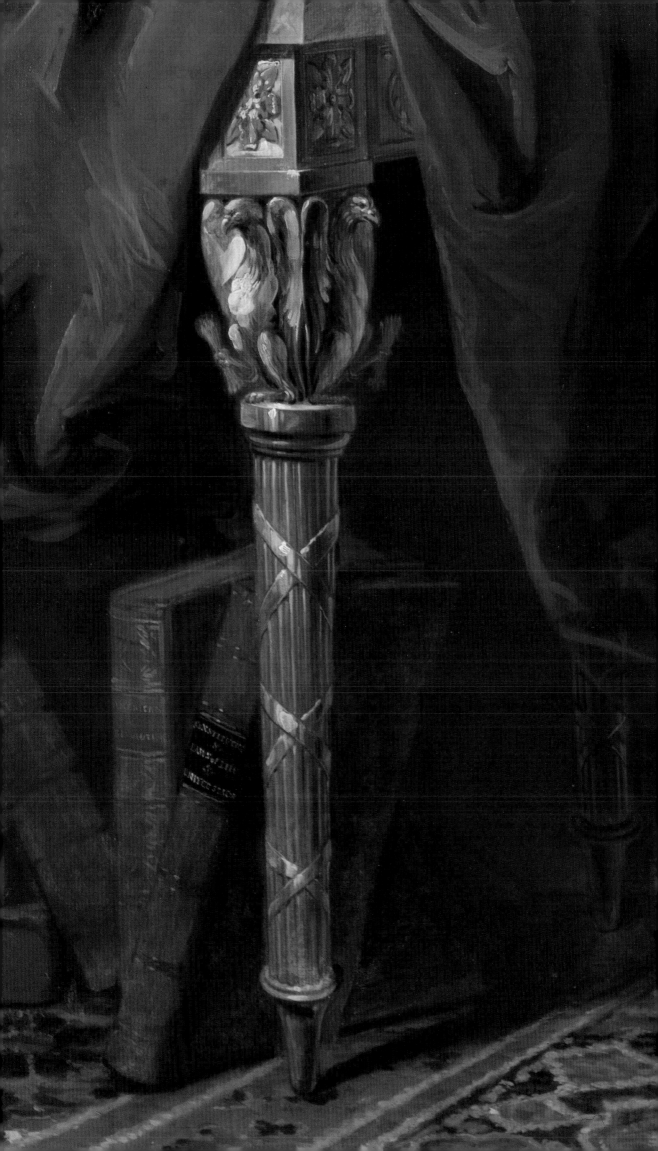

★ Gilbert Stuart's Portraits of George Washington

ELLEN G. MILES

IN 1793, THIRTY-SEVEN-YEAR-OLD GILBERT STUART RETURNED TO the United States after eighteen years in England and Ireland. While abroad, he studied painting and established a reputation as a portrait artist with particular skills at representing the individual character of each sitter. He returned to America intending to paint a portrait of President George Washington.[1] In Ireland, he had told painter John Dowling Herbert: "When I can nett [sic] a sum sufficient to take me to America, I shall be off to my native soil. There I expect to make a fortune by Washington alone. . . . If I should be fortunate, I will repay my English and Irish creditors."[2]

Born in North Kingstown, Rhode Island, in 1755, Stuart grew up in the trading city of Newport, where itinerant Scottish portraitist Cosmo Alexander gave him his earliest training in painting. He accompanied Alexander to Edinburgh in 1771, returning home after the older artist's death the next year. In 1775, on the eve of the American Revolution, Stuart's father, a Loyalist, "to get me out of harm's way, sent me abroad."[3] Stuart settled in London, where he worked as an assistant to American artist Benjamin West and attended lectures by Sir Joshua Reynolds at the Royal Academy of Arts, as well as the anatomy lectures of Dr. William Cruikshank. The success in 1782 of his full-length painting of William Grant, known today as *The Skater* (National Gallery of Art), enabled him to establish his own business as a portraitist. A contemporary reviewer wrote in 1787: "Not only skin deep, and skimming superficially over complexion and contour . . . Stuart dives deep into *mind!* and brings up with him a conspicuous draught of character, and characteristic thought!"[4] In 1787 Stuart traveled to Dublin, Ireland, with his young bride, Charlotte Coates, to paint a portrait of Charles Manners, fourth Duke of Rutland, lord lieutenant of Ireland since 1784. Stuart stayed in Ireland for more than five years, painting portraits of the Protestant ruling class with great success. He returned to the United States in 1793, arriving in New York City on May 6.

Stuart's portraits of Washington, surprisingly, were poorly documented by the people directly involved. Stuart left no known collection of manuscript material, and references to the portraits are scarce in Washington's writings. There is nothing to reveal the thought processes of the famous sitter, or the artist, or their patrons, as to who determined the poses or imagery of the portraits. Most of the documentation for the paintings comes instead from the written records of their contemporaries. These do not always agree or produce a complete picture. What follows is a piecing-together of the known documentation.

Stuart spent about eighteen months in New York painting portraits before going to Philadelphia, then the capital of the United States. He was not a well-known artist in America. As a contemporary recorded after a conversation with Stuart in 1817, "he was an entire stranger at New York. He knew however one person–& that one was Mr. Jay! . . . Mr. S. had seen Mr. Jay in London, & had painted his portrait,–& what is more remarkable, had prognosticated his future greatness."[5]

John Jay, a New York lawyer, served in the First and Second Continental Congresses and was minister plenipotentiary to Spain in 1779. In 1782 he traveled to Paris, where he–along with Benjamin Franklin and John Adams–negotiated the treaty that ended the American Revolution. He visited London briefly in the winter of 1783-1784, when he commissioned Gilbert Stuart to paint his portrait. In New York ten years later, Jay became a central figure in Stuart's plan to paint Washington's portrait. Several others who had known the artist in London in the 1780s were also key figures in this process, including Philadelphia banker and businessman William Bingham, who served as senator from Pennsylvania from 1795 to 1801, and William Petty, second Earl of Shelburne, who was created Marquis of Lansdowne in 1784, after he had served as England's prime minister. Stuart had painted portraits of Bingham and Lansdowne in London, and Jay had commissioned Stuart to paint a replica of his portrait as a gift for Bingham. (Many, but not all, of these portraits were left unfinished.) In addition, when Stuart returned to the United States, he may already have had commissions for a portrait of Washington from English patrons.[6]

In New York, Jay sat again for Stuart–this time for a portrait in his chief justice's robes–and gave Stuart a letter of introduction to Washington. Stuart went to Philadelphia in the fall of 1794 to introduce himself to the President and arrange the necessary sittings. On November 2 he wrote his uncle Joseph Anthony, who lived in Philadelphia, that he would be seeing him "perhaps in less than three weeks. The object of my journey is only to secure a picture of the President, & finish yours."[7] On November 15, Sarah Livingston Jay wrote her husband, who by then

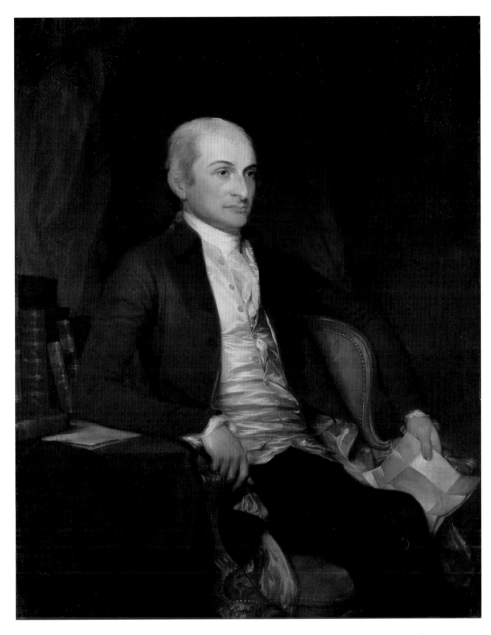

Ten years after Gilbert Stuart began (but did not finish) this portrait of John Jay in London, Jay became a central figure in Stuart's plan to paint Washington's portrait.

John Jay
by Gilbert Stuart
and John Trumbull
Oil on canvas, begun in 1784,
completed by 1818
National Portrait Gallery,
Smithsonian Institution

was in London again, that Stuart had delivered his portrait, and added that "in ten days he is to go to Philadelphia, to take a likeness of the President."[8] According to contemporary artist William Dunlap,

> Soon after his arrival in Philadelphia Mr. Stuart called on the president, and left Mr. Jay's letter and his own card. Some short time after, having passed a day in the country, upon his return he found a note from Mr. Dandridge, the private secretary, inviting him to pass that evening with the president. He went accordingly, and on entering a large room, (which he did carelessly, believing it to be an anti-chamber,) he did not distinguish one person from another of the company he found there. But the president, from a distant corner of the room, left a group of gentlemen, with whom he had been conversing, came up to Mr. Stuart and addressed him by name, . . . and, finding his guest much embarrassed, he entered into easy conversation with him until he recovered himself. The president then introduced him to the company. This incident I give from the artist to whom Stuart related the circumstance.[9]

While it is generally believed now that Stuart painted his first portrait of Washington in the winter of 1794, or, as Jane Stuart, the artist's daughter, later wrote, "toward the spring of 1795," only some of the evidence supports this conclusion.[10] It is assumed, for example, that by April 20, 1795, when Stuart compiled "A list of gentlemen who are to have copies of the Portrait of the President of the United States," he had painted Washington's portrait. The list is a record of the names of thirty-two people who commissioned replicas (as copies painted by the creator of the original painting are known). It includes several English patrons– the Marquis of Lansdowne, Viscount Cremorne (whose wife was Philadelphia Hannah Freame, granddaughter of William Penn), and artist Benjamin West–as well as New Yorkers John Jay and Aaron Burr, and Philadelphian John Vaughan.[11] This composition, which shows Washington turned to the viewer's right, has become known as the "Vaughan" type, because John Vaughan sent one version of it to his father, English merchant Samuel Vaughan, in London. Rembrandt Peale later mistakenly identified it as the original painting made at the first sittings. However, Peale, a contemporary artist who painted Washington's portrait, also reported many years later that Stuart had painted his first portrait of Washington in the autumn, not the spring, of 1795, during the same week that Washington was sitting for Peale and his father, Charles Willson Peale. Rembrandt wrote that after the Peales had their first sitting, Washington "could not sit the next day–Mrs. Washington informing me that he was engaged to sit to Mr. Stuart, an artist from Dublin, who had just come from New York for the purpose."[12]

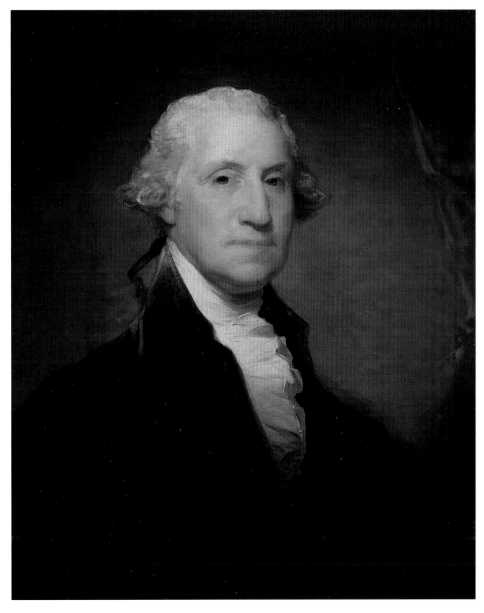

Gilbert Stuart's "Vaughan" portrait of Washington, which depicts him turned to the viewer's right, represents the artist's first concept of the President.

George Washington
by Gilbert Stuart
Oil on canvas, 1795
National Gallery of Art,
Washington, D.C.;
Andrew W. Mellon Collection

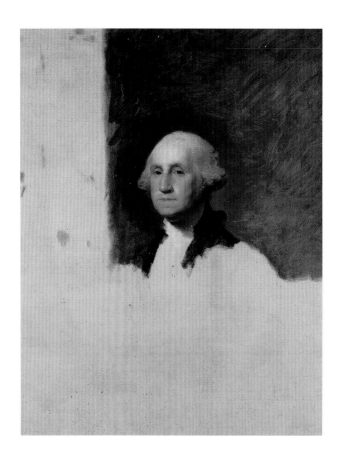

Now known as the "Athenaeum" portraits, these were commissioned by Martha Washington. Stuart left them unfinished and never delivered them to her.

———

George Washington
by Gilbert Stuart
Oil on canvas, 1796
National Portrait Gallery,
Smithsonian Institution;
owned jointly with the
Museum of Fine Arts, Boston

———

Martha Washington
by Gilbert Stuart
Oil on canvas, 1796
National Portrait Gallery,
Smithsonian Institution;
owned jointly with the
Museum of Fine Arts, Boston

After painting this first portrait, Stuart received two additional commissions to paint Washington from life; for most artists, such opportunities had become rare. One commission was from Martha Washington, for a portrait of herself as well as one of the President; these were intended for Mount Vernon after Washington's retirement. They are now known as the "Athenaeum" portraits, because they were acquired by the Boston Athenaeum after Stuart's death. In the Athenaeum portrait, Washington is turned to face the viewer's left, and Martha faces to the viewer's right, to balance the pair. None of the sittings for these portraits are documented. The only reference found in Washington's writings is an annotation in his diary for January 7, 1797, that he "Road [rode] to German Town with Mrs. Washington to see Mr. Stuarts paintings."[13] However, the evidence is very strong that Stuart had painted the portraits in Philadelphia by the spring of 1796, even though Jane Stuart believed that they were commissioned after Stuart moved that summer to "a country home in Germantown, where he transformed a barn into a painting-room."[14] Rembrandt Peale later wrote,

> soon after my return to Philadelphia, in the Spring of 1796, Mr. Stuart exhibited his Portrait of Washington. It was of the Head-size, 25 by 30 inches, with a Crimson Curtain Background–advantageously displayed in a Room of the City Hall–and was much visited, as it well deserved to be, being a beautiful work of Art.

He added, "It is here necessary to state that this was not the Portrait Mr. Stuart began in the Autumn of 1795," that is, not the Vaughan type.[15]

In his portraits, Stuart carefully sought to depict Washington so that his character would be successfully conveyed to viewers. Stuart was cognizant of prevailing theories about physiognomy, which held that the outward body reflected the inner character. When the Vaughan portrait arrived in London, it was engraved as an illustration for the third volume of Henry Hunter's English translation of Johann Caspar Lavater's *Essays on Physiognomy* (3 vols.; London, 1789–1798). This publication presents Lavater's theories about understanding a person's character and personality from the shape of the face and its individual features. The analysis of Washington's physiognomy in the text discusses this and two other engravings. The writer, who added this section to Lavater's original text, commented that "every thing in this face announces the good man, a man upright, of simple manners, sincere, firm, reflecting and generous."[16] When painting the Athenaeum portrait, Stuart sought to represent Washington more successfully than he had in the Vaughan portrait. Clearly he felt he had succeeded. Jane Stuart recorded her father's explanation of the merits of different portraits of Washington. He admired most the sculpture by French artist Jean-Antoine Houdon, probably because it was based on a life mask and therefore was the most accurate:

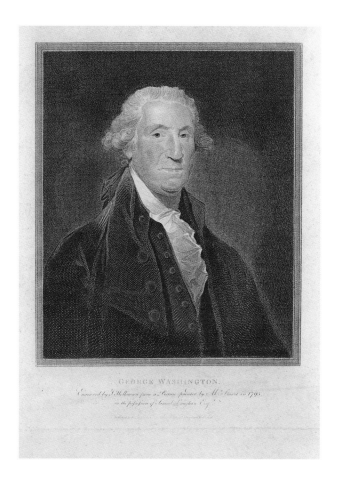

When the Vaughan portrait arrived in London, it was engraved as an illustration for an English translation of Johann Caspar Lavater's Essays on Physiognomy.

George Washington
by Thomas Holloway
after Gilbert Stuart
Engraving, 1796
National Portrait Gallery,
Smithsonian Institution

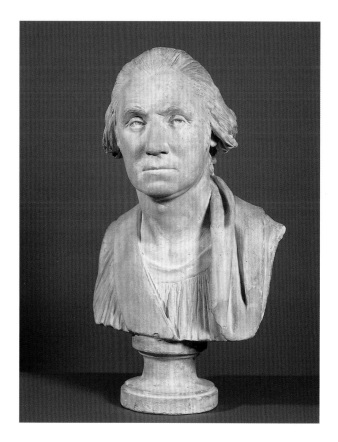

Gilbert Stuart admired sculptor Jean-Antoine Houdon's bust of Washington.

George Washington
by Jean-Antoine Houdon
Plaster, circa 1785
National Portrait Gallery,
Smithsonian Institution;
gift of Joe L. and Barbara B.
Albritton, Robert H.
and Clarice Smith, and
Gallery purchase

Houdon's bust came first, and my head of him [i.e., the Athenaeum portrait] next. When I painted him, he had just had a set of false teeth inserted, which accounts for the constrained expression so noticeable about the mouth and lower part of the face. Houdon's bust does not suffer from this defect. I wanted him as he looked at that time.[17]

Preferring this new (Athenaeum) pose to the first (Vaughan) portrait, Stuart abandoned the earlier type after making about a dozen replicas. Rembrandt Peale wrote that after "he had made five Copies of it, he became dissatisfied with [it], and requested Washington to sit for another."[18] Jane Stuart wrote that Stuart was "very much dissatisfied" with the first portrait and "ultimately erased this picture."[19] Stuart kept the new portrait in his studio, together with his unfinished portrait of Martha Washington, using the portrait of Washington to make numerous replicas throughout his life. He never delivered the portraits to Mrs. Washington, arguing that the President had told him "he saw plainly of what advantage the picture was to the painter, (who had been constantly employed in copying it, and Stuart had said he could not work so well from another;) he therefore begged the artist to retain the painting at his pleasure."[20] Jane Stuart also recorded this exchange, writing that her father told Washington that "it would be of great importance to him to retain the originals, to which Washington replied: 'Certainly, Mr. Stuart, if they are of any consequence to you; I shall be perfectly satisfied with copies from your hand, as it will be impossible for me to sit again at present.'"[21] In wishing to keep this unfinished life portrait, Stuart was following European studio practice for portraits of sovereigns and other heads of state, in which the painter would first make a portrait from life and then use it as the basis for replicas and larger compositions, including three-quarter and full-length paintings. This would have agreed with Stuart's plan to paint Washington in full-length, as he had told his Irish friend John Dowling Herbert: "I calculate upon making a plurality of portraits, whole lengths."[22]

Stuart next received the commission for his first full-length portrait of Washington. Painted for the Marquis of Lansdowne in 1796, this is now known as the "Lansdowne" portrait. According to Jane Stuart, the commission for the painting came initially from Lord Lansdowne, after Stuart had painted the first life portrait:

> Lord Lansdowne gave him a commission to paint for him a whole-length of Washington to take to England. Mr. Bingham, a resident of Philadelphia, called upon Stuart, and was very solicitous of having the honor of presenting the picture to his Lordship. Stuart, knowing the extreme fastidiousness of the English nobility, declined; but Mr. Bingham persuaded him that it would be considered a compliment.[23]

Only one sitting for this painting is documented, in a note that Washington wrote to Stuart on April 11, 1796:

> Sir, I am under promise to Mrs. Bingham, to set for you tomorrow at nine oclock, and wishing to know if it be convenient to you that I should do so, and whether it shall be at your own house, (as she talked of the State House) I send this note to you, to ask information. I am Sir Your Obedient Servt, G. Washington.

Stuart annotated the letter in 1823 that the full-length was "the only original painting I ever made of Washington except one I own myself [the Athenaeum portrait]." He added, "I painted a third, but rubbed it out."[24] This "rubbed out" painting would have been the original for the Vaughan portrait type.

★ *Imagery of the Lansdowne Portrait*

When looking at the Lansdowne portrait, it is important to understand the elaborate composition and its individual parts as representing ideas and issues of the time that it was painted. The formal pose and the scale of the portrait, as well as the use of objects to represent thematic material, are hallmarks of the tradition of European portrait painting. The size of the canvas, 95 by 60 inches, for example, was termed a "full-length" size and was used for life-size full-length paintings. These usually represented public figures, or those with the most wealth, intent on conveying their dominance in some arena–social, political, familial. The setting– a portico-like space with a wall, columns, a curtain, and an open sky behind the figure, is one that is often found in the European tradition of these so-called "state" portraits. The foreground, an ambiguous space that is often furnished and carpeted, repeats compositions used for portraits of monarchs, archbishops and other public figures.[25]

Stuart apparently relied on a European precedent for the overall composition as well. Art historians Charles Henry Hart and Dorinda Evans have suggested that the source was Pierre-Imbert Drevet's engraving of a portrait of Bishop Jacques-Bénigne Bossuet, painted by early-eighteenth-century French artist Hyacinthe Rigaud.[26] Like the portrait of Bossuet, the Lansdowne image includes an elaborate chair and table, and the pose of the figure is also similar. However, Stuart's use of an engraving was not a naive copying process. Eighteenth-century American and English portrait painters often kept collections of drawings and engravings in their studios, turning to them as references when designing the overall composition, the pose, or even the dress of a portrait. Stuart was experienced at painting full-length portraits, having created several during his years in England, and he was familiar, although perhaps not completely comfortable, with their challenges. Stuart's full-length portrait of William Bingham (see page 51),

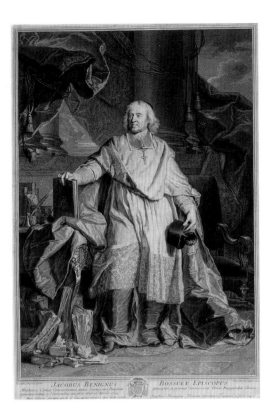

Stuart relied on European precedents for the overall composition of the Lansdowne portrait. This engraving may have been the source.

Jacques-Bénigne Bossuet
by Pierre-Imbert Drevet,
after Hyacinthe Rigaud
Engraving, 1723
National Gallery of Art,
Washington, D.C.;
Rosenwald Collection

while less than half the size of the portrait of Washington, has many of its compositional features. His Irish portraits included those of John Fitzgibbon, Lord Chancellor of Ireland (1790; Cleveland Museum of Art) and the Speaker of the Irish House of Commons, the Right Honorable John Foster. Both men are shown with the regalia and robes of office, and in addition Foster is seen "in a moment when, in the course of an address, the Speaker gestures with his left hand to emphasize a point."[27]

The Lansdowne portrait's references to Washington and the American republic differ, of course, from these European sources in specific, meaningful ways. Some pictorial elements were invented to convey meaning about the man and the times in which the painting was made, while others reflect reality. The furniture, for example, probably never existed. Its neoclassical decorative elements are derived from the Great Seal of the United States, which was authorized by Congress in 1782. The oval medallion on the back of the armchair is draped with laurel, a symbol of victory. The medallion's stars and stripes imitate those found on the Great Seal, in which an eagle bears a shield with a blue horizontal field with thirteen stars positioned above thirteen red and white vertical stripes. William Barton, one of the designers of the seal, described the stars and the stripes in 1782 as representing the thirteen original states, individually and as a confederation. Like the eagle on the seal, the two eagles at the top of the table leg are posed in upright positions and each holds a bundle of arrows—a symbol of war—in one claw (see page 76). Interestingly, unlike the eagle on the Great Seal, neither holds an olive branch, the symbol of peace, in the other claw. On the table are two books, *Federalist,* a reference to the

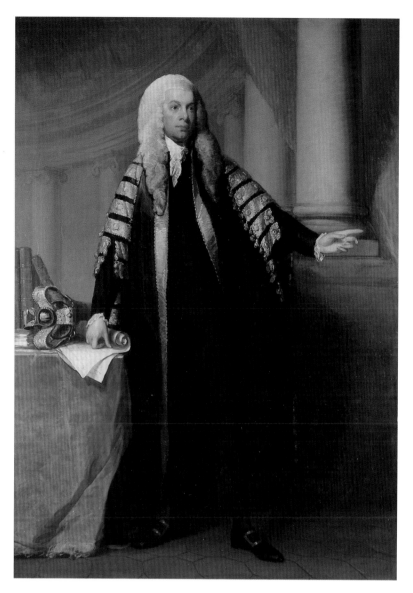

During Stuart's sojourn in Ireland, he made this portrait of John Foster, the Speaker of the Irish House of Commons. Stuart again used this state portrait tradition when painting the Lansdowne image.

John Foster
by Gilbert Stuart
Oil on canvas, 1791
The Nelson-Atkins Museum of Art,
Kansas City, Missouri

Federalist Papers, and *Journal of Congress*. Under the table are larger books titled *General Orders*, *American Revolution*, and *Constitution & Laws of the United States*. These refer to Washington's roles as commander of the American army, and as president of the Constitutional Convention of 1787, during the debates over the structure of the new government. The presence of two documents and the silver inkwell on the table could be references to the signing of a specific document, which cannot be determined easily, as neither paper has any writing on it. Stuart generally did not include such writing on documents that appear in his portraits. The silver inkwell, in the shape of an ark resting on figures of recumbent dogs, is engraved with the Washington family coat of arms. A quill pen rests in a hole in the roof of the inkwell's "cabin." Also on the table is Washington's black hat. Finally, the stormy sky and the rainbow in the background are symbolic of past storms and of peaceful times to come. When a version of Stuart's full-length was exhibited in New York City in 1798 by Gardner Baker, an advertisement pointed this out:

> Those who have not had the pleasure of seeing our illustrious Washington, now have the opportunity of gratifying themselves, and those who have seen him, will here again realize all his noble dignity and triumphs, bestowing his good advice to his country-men. He is surrounded with allegorical emblems of his public life in the service of his country, which are highly illustrative of the great and tremendous storms which have frequently prevailed. These storms have abated, and the appearance of the rainbow is introduced in the background as a sign.[28]

To compose these areas of the painting, Stuart is said to have had the assistance of architect Samuel Blodget Jr., son-in-law of William Smith, one of Stuart's Philadelphia patrons. Smith's grandson, William R. Smith, wrote in 1858: "I wish to call Mr [Rembrandt] Peales attention to the *adjuncts* to the *full length portrait* of Washington –I believe that the Books Papers, Drapery, Table, Chair &c in this Picture . . . were designed and sketched by Samuel Blodget of Philada."[29] Whether Blodget mainly helped Stuart compose the painting or whether he also helped devise some of the symbolism is unclear. The Smith family played an important role in Stuart's life in Philadelphia. William Smith, who was provost of the University of Pennsylvania, and his son, W. Moore Smith, provided the artist with residences, studio space, and commissions for portraits. While he was in Philadelphia, Stuart lived in the house of W. Moore Smith, where the sitting for the Lansdowne on April 12, 1796, took place. Later Stuart "resided in Dr Smith's old mansion on the Hill opposite the Falls" of the Schuylkill.[30]

The figure of Washington also has meaning in his pose and clothing. His face, reproduced, except for the direction of his gaze, from the Athenaeum portrait, carries with it the physiognomic meanings of that portrait as seen by Stuart and his contemporaries. Washington is dressed in a black velvet suit, the style of clothing that he wore on public occasions as President. Choice of dress was one of the many protocol decisions that had to be made for the first President. For less formal occasions, Washington wore a brown rather than a black coat. This portrait is thus a striking departure from depictions of Washington in previous full-length portraits, as painted during the Revolution by Charles Willson Peale (see page 17) and more recently by John Trumbull. Those portraits depicted him in uniform, as commander of the Continental army. This portrait instead points to his civilian leadership. Also in the Lansdowne portrait, Washington rests his left hand on the hilt of a sword. Its handle is wrapped in gold ribbon and has a gold tassel; its scabbard has a red ribbon attached with a metal buckle (see page 12). A sword very much like this one is owned by the Mount Vernon Ladies' Association. Although the sword was probably of military origin, Washington used it at this time for ceremonial purposes.

The meaning of Washington's pose and gesture, and indeed the overall meaning of the painting, is not fully documented. A recent interpretation is that the theme of the portrait is one of "benevolent governance" and that the "magnanimous gesture portends the inheritance of the future." In this analysis, his gesture can be viewed as "a greeting or even possibly a bestowal." In a somewhat timeless depiction, Washington is seen as a "paragon of virtue and, as such, a source of national pride and inspiration."[31] Contemporary descriptions of the painting, however, when read in combination with the presence of the inkwell and documents on the table, suggest that this pose was seen as having some reference to the recent signing and ratification of the Jay Treaty. This treaty, negotiated in London in 1794–1795 by John Jay, settled a number of issues left unresolved by the 1783 Treaty of Paris, which had ended the American Revolution. According to the description of the painting published in the spring of 1797 in the London *Oracle and Public Advertiser*, Washington's pose is oratorical:

> The figure is above the middle height, well proportioned, and exceedingly graceful. The countenance is mild and yet forcible. The eye, of a light grey, is rendered marking by a brow to which physiognomy attaches the sign of power. The forehead is ample, the nose aquiline, the mouth regular and persuasive. The face is distinguishable for muscle rather than flesh, and this may be said of the whole person. The dress he wears is plain black velvet; he has his sword on, upon the hilt of which one hand rests while the other is extended, as the figure is standing and addressing the Hall of Assembly. The point of time is that when he recommended inviolable union between America and Great Britain. The background is made up of a state chair, columns of the hall, and some clouds.[32]

With most eighteenth-century portraits, determining the imagery was the prerogative of the agent who commissioned the painting. With portraits of such a prominent figure as Washington, sometimes the artists designed the compositions to satisfy their public audiences. But in many cases, it was the patron who decided the theme. For example, John Trumbull's portrait of Washington, commissioned in 1791 for the city council of Charleston, depicted Washington during the American Revolution, at the Battle of Princeton. The city council rejected the painting, and asked instead for a more calm and peaceful image, showing Washington as the councilmen had recently seen him. This second portrait was unveiled in Charleston in July 1792.

If the portrait celebrates the Jay Treaty and British-American alliances, it could be seen as an example of a British practice of giving portraits on the occasion of signing treaties. John Trumbull, who served as Jay's secretary in London during negotiations for the Jay Treaty, commented on this in his letter to John Jay dated December 10, 1794:

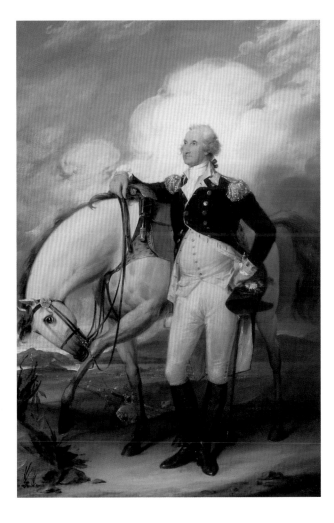

The Lansdowne portrait was the first life-size full-length portrait to depict Washington in civilian attire. As late as the 1790s, other artists, including John Trumbull, depicted him in his Revolutionary War role.

———

George Washington at Verplanck's Point, New York, by John Trumbull
Oil on canvas, 1790
Winterthur Museum, Winterthur, Delaware

Mr. Burges informed me that it was the established custom here to present to the Foreign Minister who conducted a treaty the portrait of the king elegantly set; "and on this occasion," added he, "I have by Lord Grenville's direction already given Orders to the King's Jeweller to have the picture and box which is to enclose it, finished immediately. It is also customary to make a proportional present to the Secretary of such Minister; and these are given on the Exchange of the Ratifications." I answered that I believed it to be otherwise with us, and that the Officers of the United States were even prohibited to receive presents of any kind, from any foreign Prince or State.

I submit to your Judgement how far my answer was right; and how far it was intended by the Constitution to prohibit the Ministers of the United States receiving presents of this Nature.[33]

How many times Washington posed for the portrait, and for how long, is not recorded. The usual practice for artists trained in England was at least three sittings, perhaps lasting about two hours each. The sitter's time was usually limited to posing for the face and perhaps the hands. Talented artists such as Stuart were able to paint the rest of the portrait from their imagination, or from items borrowed from the sitter. Following European practice, Stuart did not expect Washington to pose for the figure. He was, after all, a busy man, and in addition had grown tired of portrait sittings. Instead there were stand-ins. Contemporaries recorded the names of three men who might have helped Stuart by posing. One of these was "a man named Smith, with whom Stuart boarded, . . . –a smaller man than Washington," according to Washington's grandson, George Washington Parke Custis.[34] This would have been W. Moore Smith, in whose house at Fifth and Chestnut Streets Stuart painted the Lansdowne portrait. Smith's son, William R. Smith, wrote John A. McAllister in 1858:

I am glad that Rembrandt Peale recollects the fact of Gilbert Stuart having a painting room in my fathers house–the circum-stance of my Father standing for the full length figure, I conceive to be highly probable, as he was not only in the house, when, at least one of the pictures of Washington was painted, but W. Moore Smith was certainly a more graceful man in his proportions, and carriage, than Michael Keppele.[35]

However, McAllister wrote to Stuart's biographer in the 1870s that a man named "Alderman Keppele stood for the figure. I had this from his daughter."[36] A third story related that it was the Vicomte de Noailles who was the model for the figure. According to Jane Stuart, however, Noailles was involved in the completion of the portrait in a different way; he gave Stuart a "superb silver-mounted rapier" so that Stuart could include a sword in the painting.[37] Stuart may have also used casts to complete some aspects of the painting. Custis said that "the hands were painted from a wax cast of Stuart's own hand, which was much smaller than Washington's."[38]

The finished portrait was sent to London in care of Rufus King, minister from the United States to Great Britain. William Bingham wrote King on November 29, 1796:

> I have sent by the present opportunity a full length Portrait of the President. It is executed by Stewart (who is well known in London) with a great deal of enthusiasm, and in his best manner, & does great credit to the American Artist. It is intended as a Present on the part of Mrs. Bingham to Lord Landsdowne. As a warm Friend of the United States and a great admirer of the President, it cannot have a better destination. The Frame that accompanies it is manufactured in Philada. with much Taste & Elegance.[39]

When Lord Lansdowne received the portrait, he wrote on March 5, 1797, to William Jackson, Anne Willing Bingham's brother-in-law. A personal secretary to George Washington from 1789 to 1791, Jackson served as European agent for William Bingham in a real estate investment from 1793 to 1795. He noted, "I have received the picture, which is in every respect worthy of the original. I consider it as a very magnificent compliment, and the respect I have for both Mr. and Mrs. Bingham will always enhance the value of it to me and my family."[40] He ended his letter:

> General Washington's conduct is above all praise. He has left a noble example to sovereigns and nations, present and to come. I beg you will mention both me and my sons to him in the most respectful terms possible. If I was not too old, I would go to Virginia to do him homage.[41]

According to the newspaper account in the *Oracle and Public Advertiser*, "The Marquis of Lansdowne is exceedingly flattered by the present, and Lord Wycombe [Lansdowne's son, who had recently returned from America] has assured him of its perfect resemblance."[42] Lansdowne arranged to have the portrait engraved in England by James Heath (see page 64), which increased its popularity on both sides of the Atlantic Ocean. The painting itself was placed on display at Lansdowne's home on Berkeley Square in London, where it was seen in 1804 by a visitor who noted that the "full length of Washington" was displayed in the library with several statues and other paintings, including "the original model from which the statues were taken, of Sir Isaac Newton; a bust of Cromwell, full of character, the forehead very prominent."[43]

★ *Replicas of the Athenaeum and Lansdowne Portraits*

Having completed these portraits of Washington from life, Stuart again followed European custom involving such portraits of famous statesmen: he painted replicas. Scottish artist Allan Ramsay had done exactly this with his full-length coronation portrait of George III, painting numerous replicas in the 1760s for nobility, provincial governors, and ambassadors. Stuart probably painted at least fifty or sixty copies of the Athenaeum portrait, which are not signed and are rarely documented. By April of 1796 he was charging $100 for these head-and-shoulder portraits of Washington, as the young American artist John Vanderlyn reported when he worked as an assistant in Stuart's studio. Vanderlyn wrote on April 20, 1796: "I have not made any copy of the President for myself yet, but will ask his consent which if he does not object to, I will paint it before I come home. . . . Mr. S. has 100. Dolls [dollars] for a Portrait of the President which is his price for painting a likeness here[?] now."[44] Jane Stuart quoted her father on the subject of authorship of these portraits:

> My father, at this time, had so many commissions to copy the head of the President, and the anxiety to possess them was so great, that gentlemen would tell him if he would make only a sketch, they would be satisfied; and as he was painting other distinguished men of the day, and hurrying to complete their portraits, these Washingtons were, with some exceptions, literally nothing but sketches. He probably painted two at a time, that is, an hour on each in two mornings. So many people wrote to Stuart's family, after Washington's death, to know if certain heads of the President were from life, that my father was wont to say: "If the General had sat for all these portraits, he could have done nothing else; our Independence would have been a secondary matter, or out of the question."[45]

In addition Stuart was commissioned to paint several replicas of the Lansdowne portrait. Two of these are well documented. One was made for William Bingham and his wife, Anne Willing Bingham, whose country estate was called Lansdowne. Robert Gilmor Jr. of Baltimore saw this portrait when he visited Stuart in Germantown in July 1797:

Stewart came in, received us in the most welcome manner, offered us refreshments and conducting us to his painting room which he had fitted up in his stable. The Picture he had there of the President was the first copy he had made of the celebrated full length which he had painted for Mrs. Bingham intended as a present to the Marquis of Lansdown. It was supposed one of the finest portraits that ever was painted. This copy was for Mr. Binghams own use and from which Stewart told us he had engaged to finish copies to [the] amount of 70 or 80,000 Drs. [dollars] at the rate of 600 Drs a copy.[46]

William Bingham made a bequest of this portrait to the Pennsylvania Academy of the Fine Arts. The third version, now in the Brooklyn Museum of Art, was commissioned from Stuart by New York merchant and land speculator William Constable. Charles Cotesworth Pinckney commissioned another replica in September 1796, when he was on his way to his post as minister to France, for presentation to the Republic of France. However, the picture was not sent to France because the French Directory refused to receive Pinckney. This may be the full-length "Portrait of General Washington (large as life)" that Gardner Baker displayed at his American Museum in New York City in February 1798.[47] Soon after this, a version of the portrait was purchased for the United States government

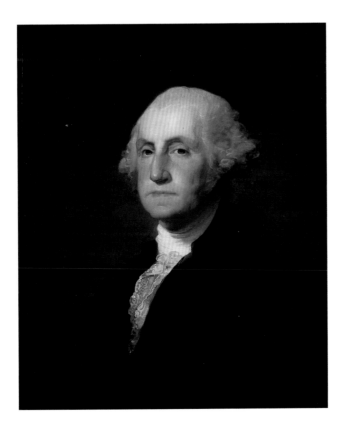

Stuart painted at least fifty or sixty versions of the Athenaeum portrait, including this one; typically, they are not signed.

George Washington
by Gilbert Stuart
Oil on canvas, not dated
The Corcoran Gallery of Art,
Washington, D.C.;
William A. Clark Collection

and sent to Washington, where it was hung in the new President's House, now called the White House. Stuart later denied authorship of that portrait, a view that some historians have continued to hold.

At some time between 1797 and 1800, Stuart painted a slightly different full-length portrait, known now as the Munro-Lenox portrait, with some changes in the pose. This change perhaps reinforces the idea that the Lansdowne pose had a specific meaning at the time it was commissioned, a meaning not relevant to the new use of the painting. He reused this composition to fulfill commissions for full-length portraits from the state houses of Rhode Island and Connecticut. By this time Stuart may have been referring to the Athenaeum portrait of Washington as "the Mount Vernon Portrait," the term he used when he advertised engravings of the new version of the full-length on June 12, 1800, in the *Philadelphia Aurora*.

> Gilbert Stuart, having been appointed by the Legislatures of Massachusetts and Rhode Island to prepare full length Portraits of the late General Washington, takes this mode to apprise the citizens of the United States of his intention to Publish Engravings of General Washington, from the Mount Vernon Portrait, executed upon a large scale by an eminent Artist.

Each subscriber would have "a full length engraving of General Washington . . . at the price of Twenty Dollars," paying half of this in advance "towards defraying the expences of the work."[48]

Stuart's training had taught him the skills and compositional formulas of the English tradition of portraiture. On his return to America in 1793, he applied these to portraits of many sitters, becoming the most sought-after, admired, and influential portrait painter in America. For more than thirty years, he dominated American portraiture with his approach to portrait painting and his personality. After painting Washington's portraits, Stuart continued to work in the Philadelphia area until 1803. His sitters were mainly the politically prominent and wealthy members of the merchant and landed classes. In December 1803 he moved to Washington, three years after the city had become the new national capital. There his sitters included Thomas Jefferson, the Madisons, the Thorntons, and others from Jefferson's administration, as well as relatives of the Washington family. In 1805

Stuart received commissions to paint several additional versions of the Lansdowne portrait. This was the first replica, made for William Bingham and his wife Anne.

George Washington by Gilbert Stuart, oil on canvas, 1796
The Pennsylvania Academy of the Fine Arts, Philadelphia; bequest of William Bingham

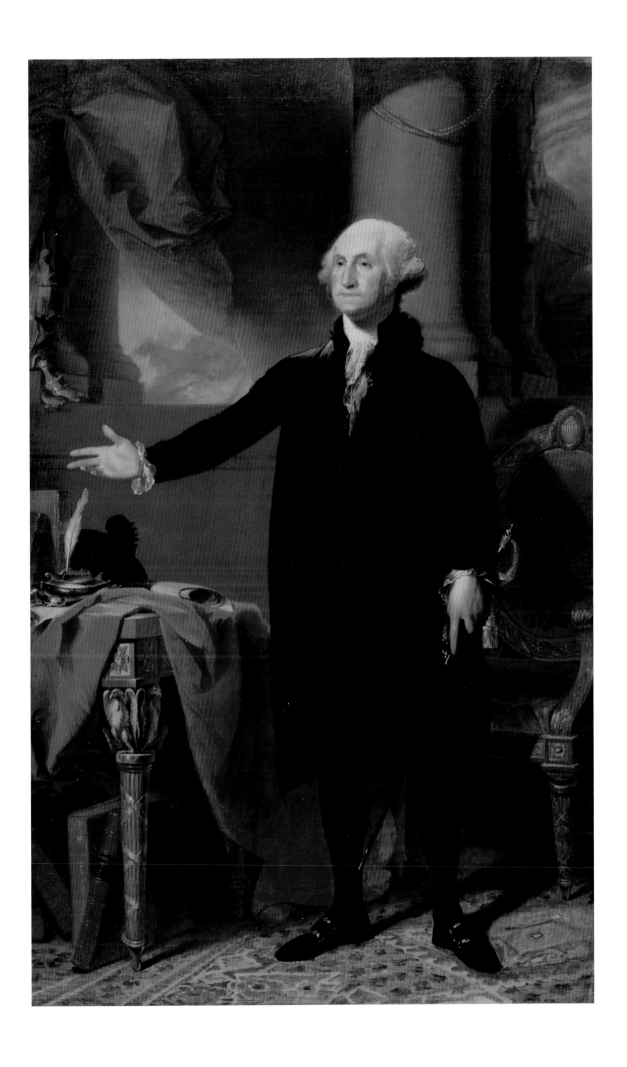

Stuart settled in Boston, where he continued to paint sitters who were politically and socially prominent. Younger American artists sought his advice and imitated his work, among them Thomas Sully, Rembrandt Peale, and Matthew Harris Jouett, as well as his own son, Charles Gilbert Stuart, and daughter, Jane Stuart. Not counting his copies of the portraits of Washington, Stuart painted about a thousand portraits during his long career. However, of all of these portraits, Stuart's images of Washington have been his greatest legacy.

Between 1797 and 1800, Stuart changed the pose of his full-length portraits of Washington, to produce the painting known now as the Munro-Lenox portrait.

George Washington by Gilbert Stuart, oil on canvas, 1800
New York Public Library, New York; Astor, Lenox, and Tilden Foundations

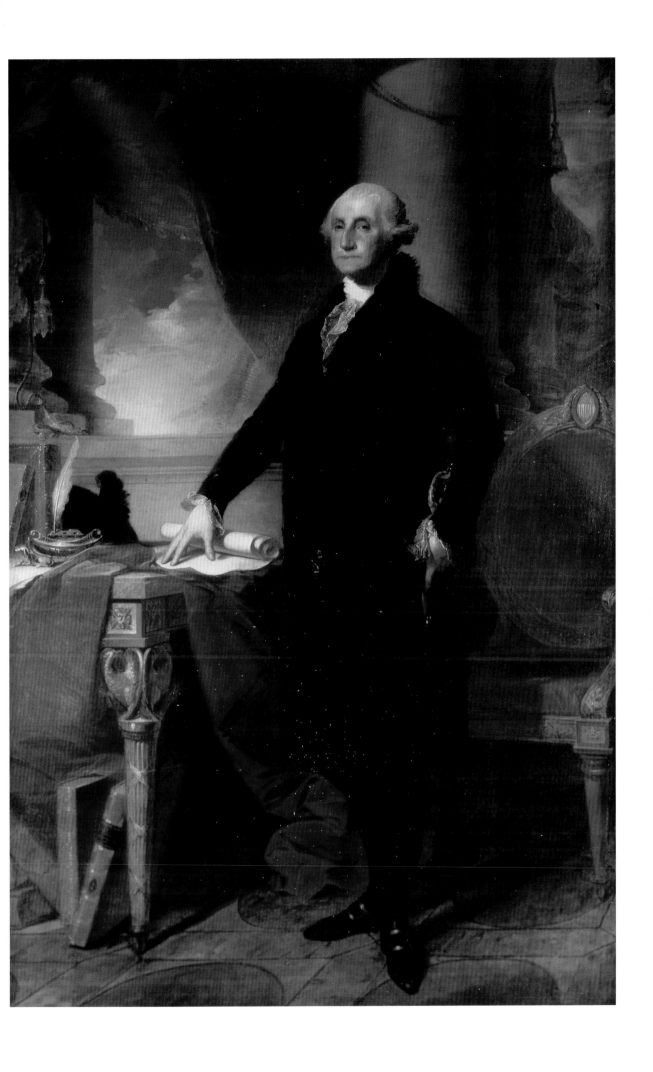

Notes

1   For other portraits of Washington as President, see Ellen G. Miles, *George and Martha Washington: Portraits from the Presidential Years* (Washington, D.C., and Charlottesville: National Portrait Gallery, in association with the University Press of Virginia, 1999). The most complete studies of Washington's portraits are John Hill Morgan and Mantle Fielding, *The Life Portraits of Washington and Their Replicas* (Philadelphia: printed for the subscribers, 1931), and Gustavus A. Eisen, *Portraits of Washington* (3 vols.: New York: R. Hamilton, 1932).

2   John Dowling Herbert, *Irish Varieties, for the Last Fifty Years* (London: William Joy, 1836), p. 248.

3   Henry Pickering, "Interviews with Mr. Stuart in 1810 and 1817," interview dated October 29, 1817, manuscript, Pickering Foundation, Salem, Massachusetts.

4   "Stuart–The Vandyck of the Time," *The World* (London), April 18, 1787, p. 3; quoted in Dorinda Evans, *The Genius of Gilbert Stuart* (Princeton, N.J.: Princeton University Press, 1999), p. 44.

5   Pickering, "Interviews," October 29, 1817.

6   According to art historian Dorinda Evans, Jonathan Mason, a contemporary, said that Stuart "returned to the United States at the suggestion of Alexander Baring and his brother to paint a portrait of Washington for William Bingham (later Alexander Baring's father-in-law)." Alexander Baring's father was a Whig politician and close friend of Lord Lansdowne. (See Evans, *Genius of Gilbert Stuart*, p. 138, n. 22, describing information in Mason's manuscript, "Recollections of an Octogenarian.")

7   Quoted in Charles Merrill Mount, *Gilbert Stuart: A Biography* (New York: W. W. Norton, 1964), p. 183.

8   Quoted in ibid., p. 185.

9   William Dunlap, *History of the Rise and Progress of the Arts of Design in the United States* (2 vols.; New York: G. P. Scott, 1834), vol. 1, p. 197.

10   Jane Stuart, "The Stuart Portraits of Washington," *Scribner's Monthly* 12 (1876): 369.

11   Ibid., p. 373.

12   Rembrandt Peale, "Washington and His Portraits," lecture, 1858; published in Eisen, *Portraits of Washington*, vol. 1, p. 308.

13   Donald Jackson and Dorothy Twohig, eds., *The Diaries of George Washington* (6 vols.; Charlottesville: University Press of Virginia, 1976–1979), vol. 6, p. 229.

14   Stuart, "Stuart Portraits," p. 370.

15   Peale, "Washington and His Portraits," in Eisen, *Portraits of Washington*, p. 311.

16   Johann Caspar Lavater, *Essays on Physiognomy, Designed to Promote the Knowledge and Love of Mankind*, trans. Henry Hunter (3 vols.; London: John Murray, 1789–1798), vol. 3, p. 435.

17   Stuart, "Stuart Portraits," p. 370. Stuart is referring to the time that Houdon made his portrait, which was in 1785.

18   Peale, "Washington and His Portraits," in Eisen, *Portraits of Washington*, p. 311.

19   Stuart, "Stuart Portraits," p. 369.

20   Dunlap, *History*, vol. 1, p. 198, recording the story from John Neagle, a Philadelphia artist who studied with Stuart.

21   Stuart, "Stuart Portraits," p. 370.

22   Herbert, *Irish Varieties*, p. 248.

23   Stuart, "Stuart Portraits," p. 369.

24   The letter, dated "Monday Evening 11th Apl 1796," is owned by Lord Dalmeny and is on long-term loan to the National Portrait Gallery.

25   As Dorinda Evans has pointed out, "Except for its specific associations, the work is consistent with a tradition of portraiture for aristocrats and royalty" (*Genius of Gilbert Stuart*, p. 67).

26   Evans writes: "The background of classical columns and tasseled drapery is a subdued quotation, via an engraving, from a more flamboyant precedent: the late-seventeenth-century portrait of a famous preacher, Bishop Jacques-Bénigne Bossuet, by the French artist Hyacinthe Rigaud" (see ibid.).

27 Richard McLanathan, *Gilbert Stuart* (New York: Harry N. Abrams, in association with the National Museum of American Art, 1986), p. 71.

28 Advertisement in *The Time Piece* (New York), vol. 2, no. 63, February 7, 1798.

29 William R. Smith to John A. McAllister, November 24, 1858, McAllister Manuscripts, Library Company of Philadelphia.

30 Ibid.

31 Evans, *Genius of Gilbert Stuart*, p. 67.

32 *Oracle and Public Advertiser* (London), May 15, 1797, quoted in William T. Whitley, *Gilbert Stuart* (Cambridge: Harvard University Press, 1932), p. 100.

33 Henry P. Johnston, ed., *The Correspondence and Public Papers of John Jay, 1763–1826* (4 vols.; New York and London: G. P. Putnam's Sons, 1890–1893; reprinted in one volume by DaCapo Press, New York, 1971), vol. 4, p. 148.

34 George C. Mason, *The Life and Works of Gilbert Stuart* (New York: Charles Scribner's Sons, 1879), p. 92.

35 Smith to McAllister, November 24, 1858, Library Company of Philadelphia.

36 Mason, *Life and Works of Stuart*, p. 92.

37 Jane Stuart, quoted by Mason in *Life and Works of Stuart*, p. 92.

38 Mason, *Life and Works of Stuart*, p. 92.

39 Charles R. King, ed., *The Life and Correspondence of Rufus King* (New York: G. P. Putnam's Sons, 1896), vol. 2, p. 112.

40 Lansdowne to William Jackson, March 5, 1797, quoted in Charles Henry Hart, "Stuart's Lansdowne Portrait of Washington," *Harper's New Monthly Magazine* 93 (August 1896): 382.

41 Ibid.

42 *Oracle and Public Advertiser*, May 15, 1797, quoted in Whitley, *Stuart*, p. 100.

43 Thomas Green, *A Diary of a Lover of Literature*, quoted in Whitley, *Stuart*, p. 100.

44 John Vanderlyn to P. Van Gaasbeek, April 20, 1796, John Vanderlyn Papers, Senate House State Historic Site, Kingston, New York; microfilm in the Archives of American Art, Smithsonian Institution.

45 Stuart, "Stuart Portraits," p. 370.

46 "Robert Gilmor: Memorandums Made in a Tour to the Eastern States in the Year 1797," *Bulletin of the Public Library of the City of Boston* (April 1892): 75.

47 *The Time Piece*, February 7, 1798.

48 For the advertisement, see Alfred Coxe Prime, *The Arts and Crafts in Philadelphia, Maryland and South Carolina*, vol. 2: *1786–1800* (Topsfield, Mass.: Walpole Society, 1929), p. 34.

★ *Index*

Photography Credits

Jamison Miller: p. 88
NPG staff photographers: cover and pp. 1, 12, 16 (Tiebout), 22, 25, 36, 43, 46, 64, 70, 71, 73, 76, 79, 82, 84
James Parcell: p. 8
Antonia Reeve Photography, Edinburgh, Scotland: p. 67

Copyrighted images
© *The Cleveland Museum of Art, 2002*: p. 66
Photograph ©1992 The Metropolitan Museum of Art: p. 20 (Leutze)
Photograph ©2001 The Museum of Modern Art, New York: p. 20 (Rivers)
Photographs © 2001 Board of Trustees, National Gallery of Art, Washington, D.C.: pp. 26, 35, 69, 81, 87
© *Collection of the New-York Historical Society*: p. 49
© *Richard Thompson*: p. 73
© *2001 The Washington Post; reprinted with permission*: p. 8
Photograph © Winterthur Museum: p. 91

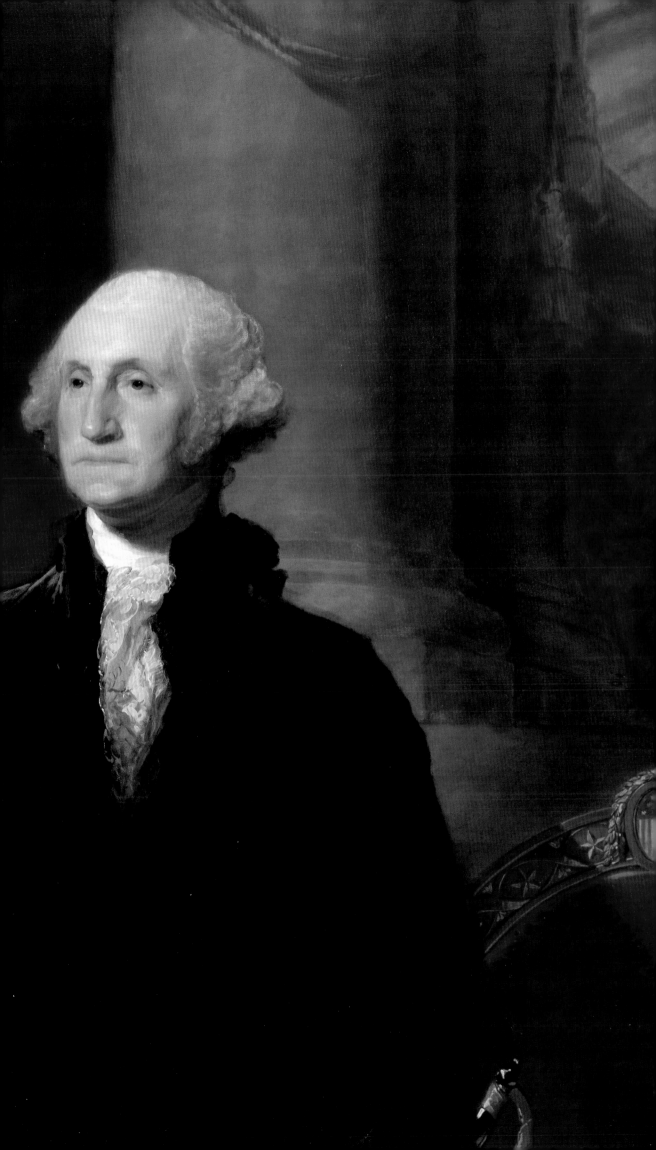